An Artist's Thought Book

Intriguing Thoughts About the Artistic Process

2nd Edition

Richard Bargdill, PhD

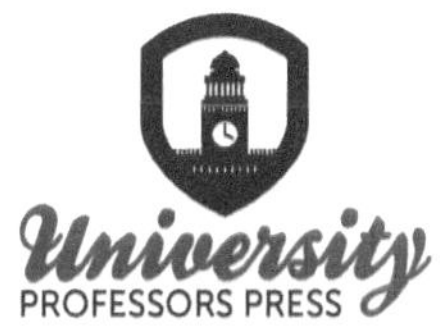

Copyright © 2014 Richard Bargdill

An Artist's Thought Book: Intriguing Thoughts About the Artistic Process
By Richard Bargdill

All rights reserved. No portion of this book may be reproduced by any process or technique without the express written consent of the publisher.

Second Edition First Published in 2014, University Professors Press.

ISBN 13: 978-1-939686-06-0

University Professors Press
Colorado Springs, CO
www.universityprofessorspress.com

Front Cover Photo by Margo DePolo
Back Cover Photo by Margo DePolo
Cover Design by Laura Ross

Bargdill's *An Artist's Thought Book* presents fascinating and psychologically-minded reflections with regard to the artistic process. Maxims are provided and elaborated upon, and readers will benefit the most from the book if they thoughtfully reflect on each maxim. Doing so will facilitate the process of artists being more meaningfully engaged with their work. I am confident that this book will appeal to musicians, visual artists, poets, and others engaged in the creative process, as well as to those whose lives are deeply touched by the arts and by creative artists.

Nadine J. Kaslow, PhD, ABPP
Emory University School of Medicine
2014 President, American Psychological Association

Richard Bargdill's book, *An Artist's Thought Book*, offers thoughtful comments on the mystery and creativity of artistry. As a singer, songwriter, and blues guitarist, I found many delightful aphorisms in this book that helped me to look at my art as well as my creative process and consider approaches from various viewpoints. The subtle humor as well as the insightful Buddhist-like chants reminded me that we as artists all suffer similar obstacles and joys along the road to creativity. A joy to read—the book can be picked up at any time, flipped to any page, and ideas will begin to speak.

Jimmy Adler, songwriter and blues recording artist of "Midnight Rooster," "Swing it Around," and "Absolutely Blues: Live at the Boneyard"

Creative inspiration can come in powerful small chunks. This book offers short insights, like seeds, that readers can ponder and let grow in their imagination. On each page there is at least one seed that will stick in your throat for part of the day!

> Eric Maisel, PhD, author of *Coaching the Artist Within* and *Secrets of a Creativity Coach*

This book is delightful, deep, risky, and fun! The artist—whether visual, musical, poetic, or a creator in everyday life—can be an upstart and a sage, a truth teller and a purveyor of extraordinary beauty. Here is a voyager who goes into new realms, risks it all and brings it back to us. In An Artist's Thought Book, through engaging maxims and selected elaborations, we get a peek into the special sensitivities of our creative seers, along with their (and potentially our own) lives, challenges, and special ways of knowing. Don't miss this fascinating book.

> Ruth Richards, PhD, MD
> Professor, Saybrook University
> Editor, *Everyday Creativity* and *New Views of Human Nature;* Co-editor, *Eminent Creativity, Everyday Creativity, and Health*

Contents

Acknowledgements

I would like to thank all the artists that I have encountered who have encouraged me—through their art—to continue working on my own projects. When the first edition of this book came out, I was deeply involved with The Ebensburg Art Alliance. This was a local group that Phil Brulia and I started more than a decade ago with the goal of talking about and showcasing art in our small community. We were able to meet fascinating artists who were doing remarkable work and we met every month for a period of five years. Then I moved to Virginia, there I was able to establish a virtual community, The Humanistic Artist, with three colleagues. This Internet group shares photos of our own artwork, exchanges pictures of works by those that motivate us, and offers various insights on creativity. I truly believe an artist becomes better with an artistic community. My gratitude also goes to Anthony Muron who helped get this book into the final form.

Finally, I'd like to acknowledge members of my family who have aided me in the journey toward becoming an artist. Margo DePolo, who photographed many pieces of my art for shows including the photographs that appears on the front and back cover. I have special appreciation for my wife, Christina, and my son, Quinn, for being supportive in those moments of darkness that all artists feel. In the pursuit of making art, I have spent countless hours toiling away in the garage/studio and I appreciate their understanding of my *local absence*. My son and I have even collaborated on a few pieces together and one of those pieces we won a small award!

Preface to First Edition

This collection of phrases, ideas, thoughts, poetry lines, and philosophical nuggets concentrates on various aspects of artistic endeavors. They include thoughts about what it means to be an artist, a poet, a painter, a singer, and the nature of creativity in general. The hope of this book is that other artists will be inspired to work more vigorously, think more deeply, and feel more determined about their own projects by reading the thoughts presented here.

Each of these statements, real or imagined, caught my internal ear as having an atypical quality to them. The unusual aspect could be in the absurd image, in an internal contradiction, in the superfluity of meaning, or in the double take of being pointed in a directionless direction. Some of the thoughts are observations, suggestions, provocations, reminders, and metaphors. Some are humorous. Others are dark. Some seem to contradict each other. Some seem so true; others are lies! In a few, the words came out backward, paradoxical, twisted, or dyslexic and were so strange that they had to be written down. Foremost, this is a book of implications, hints, whispers, and hammers. Hopefully, this volume will leave the reader with the feeling that the poetic happens on a daily basis. And more than likely, the reader also says, thinks, or hears something everyday that can be written down. Maybe they, too, will be inspired to do so.

R. Bargdill, 2006

Preface to the Second Edition

There are numerous additions to this second edition. The book is now divided into two parts. The first part is an expanded version of the maxims and so each of the first five chapters have at least 15 new maxims. These are one or two sentence thoughts that are intended as meditations on the artistic process. This means that each chapter offers 70 to 80 opportunities for the artist to pause and consider their craft building a little more deeply. You can read the whole chapter in a short time but I hope you take some time to wonder a bit about any maxim that catches your eye. You will notice as you read that a few of the maxims also have asterisks next to them. Those maxims will appear in the second part of the book with an elaboration. Those in the second half are more like aphorisms, as I have tried to write a little bit about what I think I had in mind when I wrote down the original maxim. I hope that you will read the originals first and then read through the elaborations. Obviously, when you read this book, you are free to bounce back and forth if you choose. I hope you enjoy this new format!

R. Bargdill, 2014

PART ONE:
The Maxims

Chapter 1
To Be an Artist

1

Hopefully your thoughts are sensitive—because that will make it easier to provoke them.

2

The people who are the best explorers are those who are open to the most differences.

3

The mood of the artist is often a mood of disappointment because one's vision of a project is always more pure than the finished product can ever be.

4*

The artist must continue to live on the edge of one's self.

5

Part of the reason for depression among artists is that they are always working at the outskirts of their abilities.

6

Art is really about making commitments to your self.

7

Art is about expression, not perfection—even the masters have only a few masterpieces.

8

Anger is a signal that you have come to the end of your perspective.

9

What we become agitated by is not the rejection by patrons or jurors, but by our inability to convey our ideas or concepts to people who are looking for some.

10

Not all problems of a project can be anticipated with forethought; some problems and solutions must be developed along the way. Don't expect smooth sailing after you are struck by inspiration!

11*

No matter how good an individual artist I might become, I would always be better if I was part of an artistic community. Art thrives among other artists.

12

The ability to think, coupled with the inability to work, is one of the most difficult features of being an artist.

13

No project is a waste of time even if it takes a few years to find the right accessories. Some insights have a longer pregnancy.

14

Naming an art object after an abstraction often seems to increase the ambiguity, but not the meaning or the value of the piece.

15

If you feel you already belong, you probably do.

16*

What kind of rules are you going to forgo in order to reach your goal?

17

You just have to be you until that is successful.

18

It is beautiful, if you let it be what it is.

19

Everything is a piece of art if properly
contextualized.

20

You don't need to suffer to be an artist: To be alive
means that you are going to suffer. What you have
to do is channel your suffering to open its depth, to
peer into what is already there. There is enough
pain in everyone's life already to make one a good
artist. Don't turn away from your own turmoil,
hoping for a more drastic, tragic proving ground.

21

To be original, an artist must learn to produce
chaotic work without falling into chaos.

22

The trick to being a successful artist is to make it
hard to tell the difference between your successes
and your failures.

23

I'm not talented enough to be a starving artist, that's why I'm so abstract!

24

People often suggest that one artist is copying from another artist, rather than recognizing that two artists are seeing the same thing.

25

Great art can come out of great turmoil and that is why there will always be great young artists.

26

To be an artist is to be on the margins of society.

27

May your work be so great that in a hundred years historians will claim that your work was actually the compilation of several artists!

28

The problem with thinking big thoughts is that you expect other people's minds to be opened wide enough to receive your gift. Their minds rarely are.

29*

Of course, the artist has more in common with the "psychologically troubled" person as compared to the "normal person." After all, who is more interesting?

30*

Sometimes the artist is doing the hardest work when she appears to be doing nothing.

31

Art is all a search to see one's self as beautiful. Art is the biggest mirror.

32

The amateur artist sees greatness everywhere; the great artist sees one great problem to be explored through a series of examples.

33

When your work reveals that you are in an artistic rut, just call it your latest "period."

34

Beauty is spiritual. So the artist is a spirit maker.

35*

To be an artist means to be fascinated by the insignificant.

36

You can't go chasing every artistic whim because whims will blow you around. You need to concentrate on your basic insights. Inspiration will grow deeper if you resonate with your message and find further veins of its ore.

37

Art is that attempt to articulate the self. We try to weave a story about who we are through the narrative of collected pieces.

38

The purpose of most art comes after its construction.

39

Art is seeking liberation—liberation from tyrants, self-tyrants, the past, and parents. In a way, all art is redemption.

40*

Dreams are the art gallery of the mind.

41

Art is about looking closely, seeing the folds, and seeing what was there behind and in front of your eyes.

42*

Art is getting your conscious mind out of the way of your unconscious processes; art is the craftsmanship of the unconscious.

43

You are never as far away, or as close, as you think. As long as you don't quit making art you can never fail as an artist.

44

Every art form is a delicacy that you must learn to prepare.

45*

The artist sees the cracks in the concrete of her culture.

46

Art is showing the intangible through the tangible. Great art transcends the tangible.

47*

I understand that art is the EMERGING in me.

48

You've got to realize that whichever art avenue you pick, you've got to feel good about what you're doing. Confidence is the most important ingredient in artistic success.

49

In art we sometimes run into a "problem piece." Some project we can't finish but yet can't let go of. Sometimes we've got to wait for the second insight.

50

The key is to discover what art you have the temperament for. I can sing for an hour, while I can work on a sculpture for seven.

51

Ultimately, all artistry is letting go–mostly letting go of limitations, rules, frames, self definitions, and, of course, self criticisms. So much of art is getting beyond your own personality.

52

I make all my art projects out of plastics, that way I know they will still be around in a hundred years.

53

What people become frustrated with is the work of a work of art.

54

I mostly stumble when I'm there.

55*

To be an artist means to be both a dreamer and a doer.

56

When you realize that you must take your time *here* you can now confirm you are growing as an artist.

57

The artist brings the community together; the scientist just makes it easier to be an individual.

58*

The artist tries to expand the presence of the sacred.

59

Great art forces ambiguity on the viewer and reveals
that paradox is the accurate form of truth.

60

The artists are also true martyrs of society since
none of their work is appreciated until they are
dead.

61*

If you open yourself up enough, you are bound to
become an artist; that is what an artist is—openness.

62

To be an artist might be the only way not to live life
vicariously.

63

How important for the artist to be able to say
"Ignore that discrepancy for now, we'll fix that
problem later—if it is still a problem."

64*

If failure is not near, neither is great art.

65

"Eventually right" —not "Initially right" —should be the artists mantra!

66

Is this what an artist is: a frustrated, procrastinating, drunk, troubled, indecisive, broke, unappreciated cultural laborer?

67

The artist is a resource for the community that constantly benefits from glimpses of beauty or warnings of danger.

68

Art always is revealing.

69

The artist gets a certain joy from using his body as a tool.

70*

Artistic Fallacy: I want to do something unique AND have everybody love it.

71

If you have one fan as an artist you have all you
need (even if that fan is you)!

72

An artist is at risk because at a peak moment of his
achievement he puts up his art for others to judge.

73

Each artist brings something into being that no other
artist could have.

74*

You can fail as an artist but you can never be a
failure as an artist.

75

You are an artist if you make something beautiful.

Chapter 2
Singing and Music

1*

The intentions of the song must be in the intonations of the singer.

2

Slower songs put more pressure on your vocal abilities and your self-esteem.

3

Singing seems to be similar to what they say about racecar driving. If you get in the wrong groove, the air resistance will slide you off to the side and you will have to fall back in line after several words have passed you by.

4

Singing often amounts to coming to a fork on the hilly road and choosing the high or low trail. You use your best guess the first time, and if you are wrong, you make a mental note to go the other way next time you find yourself at that note.

5

Learning to sing is like learning to hold something very delicate without crushing it. When we "pinch" the notes we have used too much force on a delicate wing.

6

The Zen of singing includes clearing your mind of external and internal factors so that the song itself and its nuances are the only and every thing present to the singer.

7

In each song there might be 4 or 5 different vocal delights that one will discover unfolding in a single song. This is what sticks in your head the next day.

8

One of the problems of using a repetitive chord patterns is the vocal arrangement must avoid becoming monotonous.

9

Singing is a system of airflow management: the sinuses, fluid intake, and of course, the control of the breath are all crucial factors in singing.

10*

Singing is a physical event; just like sports, you better practice and you should warm up before the show!

11*

The beats of a song are the rocks in the river that the vocal waters need to flow over.

12

If you like a song, do not be discouraged if your voice does not sound good singing it the first or the second time through. Do not give up on the song. It may take a while to hone in on the right vocal path just like it took a while to tune in the old knob radios.

13

You know when you've got the essence of the song when your own hair stands up while you're singing.

14

When will I trust myself?

15*

I can't find my default voice yet, which in the long run might be good because I am attempting to gain control over a number of different voicings.

16

I need a timing belt for my voice and my ear.

17

Our voice is always that central voice, default voice, or blue jean voice. It is the voice we always want to come back to: The one that just seems to feel good.

18

I think that singing is like many things, if you start slow, you will be able to detect more nuances and hear more possibilities. We have the tendency to want to go fast because we believe fast demonstrates mastery. Singing slower exposes more vocal weakness, but those are spots of misunderstanding in the song's movement. The creaks, cracks, and scuffs also can be a signature moment of a song that should not be sanitized.

19

Never trust your ears on the first hearing. It is the second time when you want to hear a song. The first is for learning; the second is for refining.

20

In order to produce certain sounds one has to turn one's mouth into a tool. "Bass" sounds come from opening the mouth, while "breathier" sounds come from pushing or flattening the mouth's plate. Ultimately, practice will allow us to pick our sounds automatically, but at least initially it may be helpful to notice what muscular movements are controlling the sounds that sound good.

21*

I have the first line to a 1000 different songs.

22

Several factors seem to be involved in the vocal potency including sleep, snot, motivation, and concentration. It is these complex interactions that ultimately help form the confident voice. Early in learning, before habit has focused the voice, the voice can appear to be completely lost one day and be back the next.

23

I'm trying to reach down and find an ancient voice.

24

The strange thing about singing is that the strong voice I had yesterday is completely gone today.

25

Try to find songs that fit your voice and tingle your soul.

26

When learning to sing, don't be concerned with how it sounds, but be concerned with how it feels.

27*

It's not that you don't know how to sing. It's that you don't know which voice to sing in.

28

If you want to find your voice, follow the emotion.

29

Remember that sound is a wave, and like a surfer, the singer must catch the wave, ride it, and exploit it. Without the singer the sound won't crash on your shore.

30*

Teach yourself to sing in cursive!

31

When will I trust myself? Would it surprise me if I found my voice at that same time?

32

I finally found the soul of the song by slowing it down.

33

It's beautiful if you let it be what it is: A simple song.

34

You have to let the song be your medium and you must simply be the chameleon who can change one's self to the emotional requirements of the tune.

35

I'm just stained by the beauty of sound.

36

God, how do you get feelings out of your fingers?

37

When you are playing at an open-mic, the goal is
not pleasing the audience. You are there for
strengthening, refining, exploring your boundaries.
People are there only for that reason. To try to
please or entertain the crowd is a chore for later.

38

I find myself longing for that song that I wrote with
a knife.

39

I need to write more songs that don't concentrate on
the "I" but on the universal places and experiences.
The goal is to write songs in which the listener is
the character.

40

I have AC/DC disease– All my songs are sounding
alike.

41

My songs always are between the absurd and
depressing—but that is a good spot.

42*

I find that when I'm writing a song, there are often two songs that are competing to get out at one time. One has to allow both to be born.

43*

A song is a piece of architecture.

44

Music, dance, song, stories, prayers, and reflection are the tried and true paths to the soul.

45

When you are working out the rhythm of a song, you need to either hold the guitar pattern or the vocal pattern constant.

46

Singing is all about confidence.

47

I'm trying to adjust my voice to the melody instead of singing a harmony with the music.

48

I'm singing with four different voices and I am comfortable with none.

49

I'm seeking out those who sing a bawdy song.

50

I need to sing with blood.

51

Just sing tragedy!

52

How free do you have to be to sing? 1000%! You have to turn yourself into the perfect tube.

53*

To sing, my soul needs to vibrate.

54

He takes his singing lessons from the garbage disposal.

55

Music attempts to give a voice to the dark corners of the mind and the crawl spaces of my soul.

56

One must remember that when one is trying to find a voice that it is quite possible that you may come across it once and then have trouble relocating it. Finding a voice is like deciding to use a flyswatter to kill a fly: Once you locate the flyswatter, the fly has also moved.

57

Sometimes the best music of your life gets erased.

58

I'm trying to get my guitar to talk to me.

59

I want to see my arm as a snake withering, wiggling, and slithering over the strings of my guitar.

60

I need to sing in the car, in the shower, in the woods —anywhere I am free—sing among freedom until you can be free among others.

61

Greatest words: "Close enough, we'll fix it in the mix."

62

A: Why do I want to sing?
B: To unleash and to liberate some deep emotion in you.
A: Then that is what my voice must do.

63

Before singing this is my new mantra: "Be Free, Be Free, BE FREE."

64

You have to get to the heart of the song even if you have to hide from it at first.

65

In music, there is always more to mine from a song.

66

You can't sing well with fear.

67

A: Little pieces of music are all that I ever got.
B: Be grateful you got a crumb.
A: Yes, a drop of music is an eternity!

68

But Mom, I'm not interested in anything BUT Devil music.

69*

Music is universal because music is an emotional regulator.

70

Artistry is inside your heart not your mind. If you can't get lost in the feelings of the music then you are caught in rational self-consciousness.

71

Let go and it will flow.

72

Give a voice to the melody.

73

You shouldn't write papers in your sleep. But, it's OK to write songs then. Keep a recorder near the bed!

74

Dreams make good song plots.

75

Life and music are the same; no matter what channel you were born listening to, you benefit by sampling others.

76

The only problem with constantly listening to the songs of others is that it can prevent you from tuning into your own music. You need your own stream of consciousness for that so you have to find your mental screen.

77

All my songs come from talking to myself.

78

I am glad everyone talks on their phones and are singing along to their music while walking down the street; now I look less crazy when I walk down the street talking to myself.

79

Everything is "just noise" to those who don't have the ears for the new music.

80*

Singing is an act of courage.

81

I want to sing the things that painter's paint.

Chapter 3
Painting

1

I had the thought that great pieces of art have to exhibit four things. They have to be:
1. Interesting- they must be eye catching.
2. Aesthetic- there must be something to behold.
3. Innovative- they often are original in technique or composition.
4. Provocative- they are meaningful in subject matter or artistic perspective.

2

You've got to do a little more than paint the sky blue to be an artist; or at least the blue must be memorable.

3*

Work on something long enough until you find a limit in it.

4

Have some fun! It will turn out all right. Your work
is hampered by veteran demands placed on a rookie.

5

Don't forget to occasionally take a step back from
your work. Most people only get within arms length
once they have been intrigued by something from a
distance.

6*

I don't like my beauty sweet!

7

The problem is you don't understand paint.

8

The paint must not just cover the surface. It must be
the surface.

9

If your painting is impressionistic, don't have a
focused object in the background while closer
things are distorted. Distortion must distort
everything.

10

With geometry, sometimes your plans can be technically right, but they still do not have the leeway you need in a practical sense. Sometimes things have to be put together with a spike.

11*

Some things will never achieve stability until you tighten the final screw.

12

When a project has multiple moments of truth you are either a good artist or a bad designer.

13

One must seek havoc all the time to find originality. Simplicity is more refreshing if you can edit your eye.

14*

You need to know color so you can forget about color! The painter must learn, practice, and explore with such regularity that eventually what took reflection is now replaced with intuition.

15

Don't become a technique—true art is not
variations on a theme but being able to vary themes.

16

Paint is like water: It can be applied in three
different forms. It can be laid down as a liquid,
sprayed on as a gas, and spread like a solid. Each
can produce different effects so that your goal
should be to become a master of the triple point of
paint.

17

A key to conceptual art seems to be to make pieces
that people don't understand and to leave those
pieces untitled so the people are pushed by their
lack of understanding.

18

It is beautiful, if you let it be what it is: a simple
vision.

19

I don't understand what technique is. That's why
my pieces are in pieces.

20

I doubt you can learn a lot from me, unless you are trying to become a less disciplined painter.

21

Don't ruin a painting because you don't want to waste some paint.

22

The frugal artist means that if one painting does not work, I paint over it. If a painting doesn't fit, I cut it up into collage. I have one painting that I work on only with left over paint. The frugal artist means that I never throw away a poor work, but sometimes I do blow them up.

23*

Let the mind fill it in!

24

It always seems to me that the studies that other artists make before they create are always made simply and without much effort. But when I try to make a study I find it to be a monumental task. My studies end up being the piece.

25

Background dance with me!

26

Give me a canvas or something to vomit on.

27

Just remember, failures count as attempts. Not everything can be a masterpiece. But all work should be pointing toward one.

28

Ideas are easy. But ideas call for solutions that are difficult. Don't be impressed with an idea until you are finished with the product.

29

The only thing that can stop you from feeling old is art.

30

I may have to face the cold hard fact that I might just be an artist!

31

The question for every artist is: Why did you pick this project and why did you pick this perspective?

32

Today, I believe that greatness consists of the confidence to believe that what you are doing is both unique and true. It means to persist when others you respect feel that you are going in the wrong direction.

33*

Painting is a lot more thoughtful than one might think!

34

I don't understand that what I really enjoy about painting is that improvisation is required.

35

To the painter, even rust is beautiful.

36*

Can you work hard enough to finish those pieces that are weak? Their weakness is their spot of greatest opportunity.

37

Plato was right! Our projects are only representations of what we have imagined in our minds.

38

Who would have ever thought that passion would be dependent on more things than just inspiration?

39

When you realize that you must take your time *here;* you can now confirm you are an artist.

40

Neurotic paintings sell more often than psychotic paintings—allow others to see themselves in your work.

41

Part of being a painter means recognizing details that have been overlooked. Being a painter is like trying to save things from "visual neglect."

42

I'm limiting all my painting to 10-hour projects. At least that last hour should instigate some spontaneity.

43

Right now I'm trying to figure out the next move
and I am not making one. I think that thinking about
it will help me avoid mistakes when I must
remember that I can always paint over them. Keep
working!

44

I like to think about painting more than I like to
engage it.

45

When painting on a surface like *felt*, make sure you
preserve something of that surface in the painting—
otherwise, you might as well paint on canvas. Make
sure the work high lights what *this* surface has to
offer.

46

I see art in things that are below art. Or maybe art
does not have the standards that buyers do.

47

To paint is to see beauty where it almost exists and
then add the one element that the scene was
missing.

48*

Sometimes it is best to leave a spontaneous painting
alone. Even a little touching up can take away the
most profound accidents.

49

Everything I work with can cause cancer. So I call
myself a "neo-carcinogenic" painter.

50

When my eyes don't work, I will paint the blurs.
When my fingers don't work, tape the brush to my
hands. If I can move at all I can create.

51

Titles should guide but not encapsulate.

52*

Floundering is part of art.

53

When a piece of art gets put on the back burner it is
because it has already lost its boil but it is still
simmering.

54

A failed painting doesn't mean you should quit, but you *should* be more radical.

55

I never understood how some people say that painting is relaxing. Every time I pick up a paintbrush I feel that I'm on trial.

56

You get 10% off that bad picture I was painting of you.

57

I never thought that being a painter might mean staring for hours at an unfinished painting.

58

If it dries the way I painted it; it might be as beautiful as I remember it.

59

Attack, attack, attack with paint.

60*

You always paint against yourself.

61

Anytime you try to paint the world some way you've missed what the locals say.

62

Even in painting you need confidence: what color to choose, what brush, how strong is the stroke. If you are painting well you are in constant motion.

63

You always learn from things you choose to paint what type of painter and person you are. Even the paint you use tells you about your personality: water color, acrylics, or oil.

64

Painting is a violent act.

65

If you don't like the painting it is not done.

66

It's not one piece that makes you an artist. It is a body of work with a few outstanding pieces.

67

If it doesn't meet your standards, don't sign it.

68

Paintings need method, content, and spirit.

69

Do you want to be the focal point of you painting?
But *Eye Joy* means there's something else to see!

70

There must be something passionate in your
painting. If it doesn't delight you, how will it be
viewed?

71

How do you know it is done? When the odds are
that your addition could just as much end up as a
distraction. That is when you sign the piece.

72

Think of your paintings as children who don't
always behave the way you would like.

73

Every error is the opportunity to improvise.

74

Sometimes there's nothing you can do but let it dry.

75

Let's ruin this or make it more of a piece of art.

76

You are an artist when you see that every splatter could be better, but prefer the imperfections of certain squiggles.

77

My mistakes were far more fortuitous than my visions of perfection.

78

Difference: You are not at a level of failure just because you are not at a level of success.

79

Art happens in real time. Use trusted tools like pens and paper to capture the idea. If you depend on technology to record something, it could be updating itself.

80

Every time I go to throw away a piece of art that I have deemed to be no good, I seem to find something sublime in it; so that I decide that it is not as near a disaster—even though it is not a masterpiece.

81*

New Motto: Do it! Screw it! Fix it!

Chapter 4
Poetry

1*

What makes language a poem is the deliberate beauty of each word in context.

2

A thought is a small sentence. A poem is a short stream.

3

A: I haven't written in so long, now that I am writing, I think everything I am writing is worthy.
B: That will wear off.
A: Yea, I quit writing when I thought everything sucked.

4

Poetry attempts to alter the landscape of meaning by revealing what was under the surface of the mainstream.

5

Poetry is the pursuit of the profound.

6

Why is description so artistic?

7

Oftentimes, people believe that they might not write another poem. But poetry is not one of those things that flee from one's heart.

8*

The poet's mouth must have free access to the stomach, heart, and mind.

9

Being a poet means trying to articulate what one lives.

10*

Poems are not really to be experienced auditorially but rather in the flesh. I want to feel your poems on the back of my neck.

11

When you are trying to say something and the words miss the mark—this is the sign of a poem present. Often the first phrasing is not complete but does reveal there is something that has potential for verse.

12*

Having a life poem—versus not having one—will determine whether a nice bottle of wine turns into a beautiful one.

13

If you think you have the first good line for a poem, remember it can be the first, but also last or middle line!

14

When you can't get any more material for a poem or a song, it is because you have lost contact with the voice that is trying to speak. One must try to re-enter the voice and speak only what it tells you.

15*

Pain without meaning is trauma. Poetry makes pain meaningful.

16

My personal notebooks are a cauldron of bubbling thoughts, poems, prayers, dreams, and songs that should be a mind-bending concoction—a witches' brew—for those who think straight.

17

Compared to the psychotic, the poet has slightly tighter loose associations.

18

It is beautiful, if you let it be what it is: a simple poem.

19

I'm downsizing this poem. I'm giving a few of the stanzas the pink slip.

20

Sometimes your elixir outlasts your poetry.

21

The work of poetry is resisting the urge to put in clever filler. A great line is only great if it must be there.

22*

The truth is found between the first and second draft. You never say what you think you say when you first say it.

23

Poetry is about training yourself to be able to say what it is that you have to say when you have something to say.

24

You have to find an example in language before it finds an explanation in you.

25

Poetry doesn't seem like it is appropriate in hot weather. Poetry needs a cool breeze and evenings. There has to be a 'lightness" to the body that allows the ears the ability to lock on to meanings; poetry is like that distant radio station one can tune into only on a cloudless night.

26

Why do poems come when I'm in a hurry? Poetry appears at the periphery and tests your commitment!

27

I've been to places where I could not ever be in a
position for poetry. But luckily, other poets could.

28

Oftentimes when something great or something
tragic happens you will hear people say, "I can't
really describe what I feel." Being able to put
significant moments into words is the job of the
poet.

29

Why is description so artistic? It shows and does
not tell.

30*

An author's greatest achievement is not that the
reader understands her intentions, but that the reader
is sparked to thoughts of his own.

31

Your hearing is bending my words.

32

There's gravity to our lives because we give weight
in the form of meaning to the individual moments
of our lives. When we articulate that meaning it is
poetry.

33

My words turn into little punks after they drop out
of context.

34

Everyone should memorize at least one poem.

35*

The reason for writing down a thought is to free
your mind for the next one (instead of concentrating
on remembering the last one).

36*

Every word is a junkyard.

37

Poet: If I have a gift, I have gifts with words.

38

That was so vague and unscientific that it must have been poetic.

39

I guess they outlawed Absinthe because it made the poets crazy and that's the last thing the government wants.

40*

You don't set out to be a poet; you earn the right to be one. You end up a poet because you've been blown open by the explosive perspective of words.

41

Good writing means that the reader can interpret the words the way you meant them AND the way they find them.

42

Everything that slips from your mouth is a piece of poetry. Everything that I construct is a piece of plaster!

43

I like to do a lot of writing in the dark; that way, the
handwriting matches the content of the dark
thoughts.

44

I've got sticky ears for profound things said. I've
got flypaper for your pesky phrases.

45*

Reading, Writing, and Reflection are the three paths
to improving one's mind. If you want to sharpen
your mind you have to rub it against something
abrasive.

46

I see the beauty of reading things twice. The first
time I underlined all the wrong things!

47

I could no longer follow the smooth curves of her
conversation. I slipped off into love.

48

Whenever I'm writing and trying to say one thing, it
never gets there–I seem to only be able to say two
things at a time. Writing is often about twins.

49*

A made metaphor means a new species has moved into our language gene pool.

50*

Who needs toys when you have language to play with?

51

I can only fit a few thoughts in such a short sentence.

52

Poetry is like putting in golf: speed and direction are the most important reads.

53*

The mind of the poet was meant to wander.

54

A poet is anyone who is deliberately playing with language to expand the consciousness of human thought.

55

You have to find an example in language before it finds an explanation in you.

56

We must liberate ourselves from the language of the actual.

57

Language is a puzzle with a million pieces.

58

Poems are created to capture the beauty of an event and to sprinkle it with language—verbally gift-wrapping that which might go unnoticed.

59*

Bandaged with words: Poetry has healing powers because it encapsulates the emotional shrapnel and gives it form.

60*

The poet's job is to make the public feel what they miss when they watch the tragedies at six.

61

I like that poet! She is like a metaphorologist.

62

I mostly say what I don't think. Occasionally my words and thoughts line up. I call that poetry.

63*

Poetry is finding joy in the ambiguity of language.

64

Poetry is the most affordable of the arts; that is if you can get "free" silence.

65

The poet has to know the gist of what she wants to convey and then has to ride on the wing of meaning.

66

The poet is the liberator of language.

67

Poetry is more like a cat than a dog. It comes when it wants to and not when you call.

68

Language is not a limit! Language, itself, is living!

69

Writing things down is an attempt at immortality!
Who said that?

70

Sharing your nighttime dreams is the beginning of
poetry because when you turn those images into
words, you realize how much you select your
reality.

71

When you chew life, you get meaning. The poet
talks with his mouth full.

72

Language doesn't want to be written down. It
wants to run free thorough your head like a wild
beast. To write is to capture a thought and to lock it
into place much like a photograph freezes an animal
on the prowl. Luckily, language is a chameleon.

73

With texting we see culture's direct effect on language. If you charge per letter, the language changes to a minimalist code.

74

The job of the poet is to put words in awkward situations.

75

Was that a poem or a language fire?

76*

The stories that you tell over and over are the poems you are being called to write.

77

If your thought rings for the culture, you are a successful poet.

78

A poem you know by heart is a prayer.

79

Blessing: Sometimes you get an entire poem out of a single typo.

80

Emotion must be released for meaning to be made. Poetry is a therapeutic.

81

I belong to language.

Chapter 5
Creativity

1

Creativity is a renewable well. We don't have to worry that we will use it up as long as we use it well.

2

Everything I do is an experiment rather than anything that results in the truth.

3

Future beauty is tripping you now.

4

Discovery is always an orgasm.

5

Remember that your educators don't have to be human.

6

You try to add random into everything when that is exactly what you want to subtract.

7*

Just remember that most experimental failures are seen as "turning points."

8*

Inspiration is seeing pure possibility.

9

Creativity needs both inspiration and will; all else is distraction.

10

Life is not about having talent but allowing talent to have you.

11

To become creative means to succumb to the beauty and tragedy of life on a daily basis.

12*

All creativity is the articulation of something that wants to be seen.

13

People feed on the emotion of poets, painters, and other creative-doers because to feel deeply is to risk feeling pain. People prefer to risk by living vicariously so every artist is a pioneer.

14

You can't punch a piece of art enough times to make it right.

15

An artist needs to be like every good whore— desperate every day.

16

A civilization is in decline when its creativity turns into negativity.

17*

Creativity is a constructive path to the future.

18

Most great thoughts are thought alone.

19

My inspirations lack focus. When I start to "see," I also start to "hear" and "think." I paint one day—only to be inspired to sing the next day—then to write the following day. Suddenly, life interrupts and "POOF!" I don't remember what I was thinking about. I can only interpret the fragments, like some archaeologist with a hangover.

20*

To be prolific means to have low standards!

21

Reflection is one route to creativity. Sometimes asking: "What is the meaning of this project?" or "What it is going to amount to?" is hurtful to the project. Reflection can stop action whereas passion can run right through the stoplights.

22

Because of the anxiety of life, Freud recognized that there is a "patient" in each one of us. However, the existentialists argued that our handling of anxiety can provide the opportunity for each of us to be an artist.

23

Inspiration needs a container or it will all end up on the floor.

24

Is it a surprise that periods of creativity are also periods of great anxiety? When we see possibilities, but question our ability to reach them, we experience anxiety, which is either transformed into creativity or into illness.

25

All work is put forth as a result of only a few moments of creativity and exploration.

26

An infection control team arrived because they heard I was having an outbreak of the imagination.

27

Creativity means constantly fighting habit.

28

Creativity is not just a moment; it is sustained work. Even if the idea is clear and the kernel appears as the whole gestalt, the thing has to move from the mind to the product.

29*

The significant people in your life are your muses.

30

Truth's most profound size is a kernel.

31

Passion, discipline, and confidence are parts of my triarchic theory of creativity. Passion means to allow oneself to be moved by inspiration. Discipline means to work on the project after the high of inspiration has worn off. Confidence is the belief that this art product needs to be born and I am just the person who has been asked to birth it. I do have the abilities to pull this off and it is a worthy project regardless of other person's praise or condemnation of the finished outcome.

32

Intuitive work is great for creativity and discovery while meticulous work is needed for completing the project and keeping records of the process of discovery.

33*

Remember that when you trip you are usually in between steps.

34

Greatness has always been stolen.

35

Only a good artist knows what and how much to steal.

36

All the beautiful unknown women in my dreams must be my muses. But what are they trying to tell me with their kisses? Why tell me in my dreams and not in reality? It is not time yet! I still have growing to do.

37*

In our culture when we feel inspiration, we take Pepto-Bismol.

38

Creativity: What sort of torture is this?

39

It's not education we need; it's inspiration. I was educated but I got over it.

40

Can you transcend the love of your favorite artist?
We begin by mimicking them, but imitation
becomes dead weight. We need to only sample
them and not live in their shadows. If we do not
break free, then we do not develop our own
standards or speak truly to our times.

41

My muse is on strike! What are her demands: that I
become more observant, that I be less critical, that I
be more reflective? Won't she just take some
money?

42

The inspiration usually wears off about the same
time I realize that the project requires more skill
than I now have.

43

Even inspirational moments must be managed! I
frequently get my inspirational ideas in the middle
of the night. Then, I spend several hours thinking
about them and I am unable to return to sleep until
just before I have to wake. When I get back to the
work, I am so exhausted that my work is of
mediocre quality. The difference between creativity
and mania is that creativity can be paused.

44

A bout of inspiration is like a bout of drinking. It can only go on for a limited period of time. Then there will be a crash and a period of recovery before the next case. Hopefully, there might also be a period of reflection about both incidents.

45*

We often think that passion is something you find or tap into rather than something you generate.

46

Invite creativity and it will come. Nighttime dreams show that creativity will come even without invitation. But why make it knock?

47

Passion is a blindness: to be so emotionally focused as to not be distracted by what the culture would prefer you to concentrate on. This all encompassing focus allows the artist to envision something that the world will later recognize in itself—once the artist shows that it was there all along.

48

Has my middle class-ness, my conforming society, the normalcy of my upbringing so infected my mind that I have become a passionless person? The only hope is to recognize that you are a commodity of a culture. That is the ground of Being. Your self-construction begins now!

49*

Even artists must remember how to play.

50

How many times have we confused the adjective "crazy" with the adjective "passionate?" The borderline between the two is very porous because passion does not want to keep to the boundaries of its container.

51

We tend to think of passion as an emotional experience rather then the total package of interest, practice, knowledge, analysis, imagination, and determination.

52*

Never to let the truth get in the way of your imagination! Truth is always a post-hoc evaluation.

53

Probably the worst traumas that happen to us…occur in our own imagination.

54*

I was only the key holder for a moment.

55

Hollywood is going to need a bigger net to capture my imagination.

56

It's only a porthole to the imagination if something comes out the other end.

57*

Holding other people down is never a road to creative superiority, or superior creativity.

58

Creativity is spawned by the frustration of a problem unsolved.

59

My Muse has a focusing problem. Her tangents have tangents. But if I give her Ritalin, she might talk straight but lose her poetry and wouldn't I go from creating to following a technique?

60

Life is beautiful today. I'm glad it doesn't appear so every day. Constant beauty eventually gets overlooked and then ugliness becomes pretty.

61

You are young and have an appreciation for beauty. I'm old and have an appreciation for peculiarity.

62

You can't turn away a visit from the muse even though she shows up at inconvenient moments.

63

You have a vegetarian imagination; everything is fresh, crisp, and low in fat

64*

Each day you should have at least one thought that is worth writing down.

65

That was either profound or it was hyperbole.

66

It is a great idea if you become enlivened.

67

The artist has to hold on to the power of possibility and resist the forces of criticality.

68

It is beautiful if you let it be what it is: a simple insight.

69

Inspiration is a flashbulb off a camera; it is brilliant and stunning but fades quickly. Run for your pencil.

70

Sometimes your scribbles are the message.

71

Artists should never assume they will be rewarded for their sacrifices.

72

You want to bring ambiguity into the picture.

73*

Creativity's death is boredom.

74

How have I come to the passions? Have I been able
to add to the bodily desires for food, drink, and sex?
Have I found the discipline to allow the other
passions such as intellectual, artistic, and spiritual
ones, the room and the protection to grow—that all
young things need?

75

Editing is the same as giving something another
coat of paint—you get closer to your intention.

76

Dreams are hard to remember and creativity is often
inconvenient—make time for both!

77

Where is the passion? Do not confuse it with greed,
lust, or recognition; they are by-products, possibly
even ends. Passion can never be authentically
motivated by the ends.

78

I guess we can't expect Muses to speak English.

79

You can't wait for inspiration you have to simmer
it.

80

I need a spiritual oil change.

81

Creativity is the sacred!

82

Occasionally even the rivers of creativity get
damned up and in that dry season one might believe
nothing will flow again. These are the thoughts
before the flood. What cracks the damn is your
desire for it.

83*

Invite it! Welcome it! Enjoy it! Thank it! (repeat)!

84

You've got to learn to be **a better antenna**. If your
work is the product of artistic inspiration then you
have to take your transmissions and learn how to
fine-tune your receiver!

85

So what is always rapping at your door?

Part Two
Selected Elaborations

An Artist's Thought Book is a series of maxims—one sentence to two sentence thoughts—that are roughly categorized into five chapters. It contains thoughts about: what it means to be an artist, poet, singer, painter, and also includes thoughts about the nature of creativity.

In this section I will elaborate on some of the maxims so that they become more like aphorisms. The purpose of a maxim is to say enough to provoke thought in the reader without completely spelling out what the author specifically means. By dividing the book into parts, readers have had a chance to contemplate their own meanings for the maxims contained in the first five chapters. In the following chapters, I have picked a few of my favorites and will try to describe what I *think* I was thinking when I wrote them.

Chapter 6
To Be an Artist Elaborations

#4

The artist must continue to live on the edge of one's self.

There is a tendency to believe that the artist needs to develop a signature style that other people may easily recognize. I'm sure that this is helpful for marketing since similar artwork is consistently paired with the artist's name. For growth to exist (or prosper) in the art itself, the artist must resist, to some extent, becoming a motif. Many of the great artists go through periods of "reinventing themselves," which almost always leads to fresh material. In music, this might mean the folk singer tries to write country songs or religious songs as Bob Dylan did with varying degrees of success.

If there is no anxiety present in a piece of work there is probably also little passion. The projects that I have been most proud of are the ones that I was unsure would work at all. I've had a few sculptures that seemed like they might not be physically able stand up when completed. Luckily, they did. It seems that the success of one project and the self-esteem that comes from it are exactly the resources that must be put at risk in the very next project. It is the possibility of failing that often spurs on the creative insight.

#11

No matter how good an individual artist I might become, I would always be better if I was part of an artistic community.

Often times the artist is portrayed as a resilient loner who spends all of their time in a studio or basement. The need for time and space is true to some extent. There are many tedious hours of working, once the inspiration burns off. However, if we look at many of the great movements in art, we will find that most of the cutting edge stuff happens when groups of artists, writers, and philosophers gather together and there is an interplay and even friction of ideas. In fact, it is surprising how much art has been influenced by things like philosophy and physics! One way to make yourself a better artist is to get out of your studio. We must talk to other artists, read stuff that is difficult, and create a community where artists can gather to play.

#16

What kind of rules are you going to forgo in order to reach your goal?

Every art form requires that the working artist learns some of the basics or fundamental rules of the medium that the artist is working in. Probably everyone can produce a beautiful piece of art without knowing much at all. But to consistently work and build a collection of pieces, one is going to need these fundamentals. It might also be wise to take note of the fundamentals or finer points that strike you as being backwards. These odd rules become an opportunity to explore a series of paintings or poems that attack this status quo. Art is inherently rebellious in nature since it values unique thoughts and fresh perspectives. But this means that we as artists face our greatest challenges in overcoming ourselves. Often it will be our own selves who put the limits on our own abilities. We will make false claims like "I'm not good at drawing hands" or "I can't really describe what I am trying to get at." In order for us to grow as an artist, we have to be able to also attack both our medium's rules and our own.

#29

Of course, the artist has something in common with the "psychologically troubled" person! Compared to the "normal person"—who is more interesting?

Illness, artistry, and normalcy can each be evaluated on how personal meaning in life is in harmony with the meaning of that person's culture. In illness, there are disorders of surplus meaning such as paranoid schizophrenia, anxiety, and sexual paraphilias. Here people find excessive meaning that is not shared by others. They become alienated because they value meanings that others see as peculiar. Then there are illnesses that have a deficiency of meaning such as mood disorders, catatonic schizophrenia, anti-social disorders, and addictive disorders. Here, the person does not see meaning where others do and they do not participate in a safe level of cultural standards. In both cases, there is an extreme clash between the person and the culture that typically leads to imprisonment, psychiatric treatment, social exile, or death.

The "normal" person sees meaning in culturally defined ways and in a ready-made fashion. They follow the grooves in front of them. Their struggles can still lead to discovery, but often the discovery is more on the level of fact rather than that of epiphany. The status quo has either been good to them or they cannot take the risk of trying something different.

The artist (hopefully) sees meaning outside of the culturally defined ways and is able to point out to others (the normal and the ill) the possible meanings that are hidden, latent, or emerging from the culture. The artist is a cultural commentator, an imaginative leader, and, most of the time, an explorer on the periphery of their culture. The artist is rarely successful in the generally valued ways of the culture, such as riches and power. The artist holds the unusual position of often directing the culture, but not benefiting from this directing; therefore, the artist's ability to create meaning for one's self and others is the greatest human commodity.

#30

Sometimes the artist is doing the hardest work when she appears to be doing nothing.

Much of artistry is simmering, gestating, and waiting. Waiting for ideas; waiting for parts of the composition to come together; waiting to trust yourself as an artist; waiting for others to see your artistic merit; waiting for discovery; waiting to discover that you really wanted to remain a starving artist; and, like it or not, sometimes you have to wait for the paint to dry! Thus, art does take patience, even if anger is part of it. Insights come only when you are working on a problem but usually not when you are directly thinking about it. You have to think about it, so it will come later. If you call for it, it will come, but it won't arrive immediately after beckoning. Apparently, insight is slightly slow of foot.

#35

To be an artist means to be fascinated by the insignificant.

I've heard people say, "Great art needs a great subject." Certainly, this is true on one level; however, I often feel that the artist is better served operating on a much smaller scale: the overlooked. We all feel a sense of beauty staring at a great subject like the Grand Canyon, but I think many artists can become side tracked by trying to "write the next great novel." Instead, an artist who attempts to see beauty in the small things, the things that most people pass by, is an artist who is opening the eyes of one's culture. Opening up one's self and others to the possibility of beauty is a primary goal for artists.

#40

Dreams are the art gallery of the mind.

I had this dream that I was in an art show. I was walking through the gallery looking for my piece of artwork. As I was walking, I looked admiringly at the talent of those other artist's work. It seemed to me, in the dream, that each of the artist's works contained more beauty and deeper symbolism than my piece had. I had to view a lot of art before I finally found my piece. I stood there and looked at it for a second. It was a good piece. I felt a sense that my work did belong in this show and I was making a contribution. When I woke up, I started to think about this dream. I realized that I didn't recognize the art on the walls as being the work of famous artists such as Picasso or Van Gogh, nor were they the works of people I know. I came to see the works of some unknown artist and that artist was me: *every* painting on the walls of that gallery was *mine*. My unconscious had created the artwork in my sleep and I liked it. Now, in addition to pen and paper I keep a sketchpad next to my bed.

#42

Art is getting your conscious mind out of the way of your unconscious processes: Art is the craftsmanship of the unconscious.

It seems that so often what stops the artistic process is *thinking*. When we think, we judge, criticize, procrastinate, or even worse: play it safe. The best ideas that I get for my artwork generally happen when I'm doing something completely unrelated. When doing so, I get this "aside thought" about an art project. For me, art ideas do not happen because I want them to happen; most of the time they happen in spite of me. They happen unconsciously (or at least automatically). The most important thing is to recognize any idea as worthy of writing down or sketching out. Probably the worst habit is to "evaluate" the worthiness of the idea before making notes on it—because evaluation is a conscious task and it will frequently tell you that the idea is "a waste of time," "not that unique," or "too difficult." We have to learn how our own unconscious processes work and then put ourselves in the position to receive what it delivers. Write down your thoughts and you can always come back to them. Some thoughts age well and some thoughts don't. Something that doesn't seem profound today might become profound in a couple of years. Write them down.

#45

The artist sees the cracks in the concrete of her culture.

An artist is a social commentator in almost the same way as a journalist or a politician. The artist reflects in the subject matter something about the world from which they come. An artist shows the viewers what has captured the imagination of one of their individuals. An artist holds a mirror up to the world where a wound lies or where a crack exists in the concrete. In that crack, the artist plants a seed in which something can grow that will continue to reveal the culture's needs.

#47

I understand that art is EMERGING in me.

It is often difficult to identify oneself as an artist because that title seems too concrete—too noun-like. If art is anything then it is a verb, or a process, and thus it might help us to describe one's self as "art-ing" much like we call ourselves human *be-ings*. In any case, this aphorism is intended to draw attention to the artistic process, which often requires some time to boil. The arting process means that a person has become sensitive to everything that brings a smile, a frown, or a turn of the head. All idiosyncrasies are noted and put into the cauldron of the imagination. While this amalgamation of observations is allowed to churn, stir, and simmer through unconscious processes, it will be the conscious mind that ultimately tastes and decides to pursue the project that the inspirational stew has produced. Everything *can* be fuel, but it must be the artist who provides the psychological and mental energy to ignite the fire. Emerging means the artistic process often contains self-conflict and consternation—both are good sources of mental fuel. They lead to questions such as: Why is this no good? How can I take this to the next level? What is there left to paint? Why is there no majesty in my subject matter?—all push that emerging process. Answers will come to those questions. We have to be ready, open, and able to recognize the answers as such. This will be difficult since they will not look like the answers we have traditionally received.

#55

To be an artist means to be both a dreamer and a doer.

To be an artist means to posses a number of characteristics that are difficult to combine in a single human being. An artist has to be able to play and work; play with ideas and let them go where they want to go and imagine slight or drastic variations to all of the parts. Play means to have do-overs and the sort of freedom that allows for all kinds of rule bending and experimentation without criticism. On the other hand, the artist has to show up for work. One has to often set aside time (unless one is a professional artist) to work on projects and have the discipline to be convinced that the project is worthy of the time, money, and effort that will eventually bring the project to completion. In addition, there is a certain psychological toughness that the artist needs to persist in the face of unlikely odds of success. Some other aspects of this include: the desire to make a meaningful contribution to culture; an openness to see layers of meaning where others see no complexity; the fearlessness to produce work that everyone will think is really about you. In general, this means having the ability to take psychological risks of owning thoughts, ideas, and products that might clash with the status quo of your culture. If you can see conflict, paradox, and/or inconsistency in the human soul then you can be an artist. You will also need to play and work.

#58

The artist tries to expand the presence of the sacred.

The presence of beauty *is* the sacred. The sacred is the presence of beauty. We only have a few "touching moments" in a long life—these are sacred moments. We have to live in the absence of the sacred or with the hope that the sacred will return. An artist comes to recognize this and seeks out the sacred, trying to be in a position to capture a few extra appearances. Ultimately, she also attempts to produce the sacred for herself and others.

She only has a few indications of the sacred's presence.

There are physical signs that come with the feeling of awe. We say, "Wow! That took my breath away;" "That gave me chills;" or "My eyes welled up." Whatever the sign, it is an authentic experience. This is what the artist hopes to give to you. Of course, this is becoming increasingly difficult in a world that is more and more artificial and pre-packaged, which makes the sacred hard to stumble upon. The artist is also a re-introducer of the authentic.

#59

Great art forces ambiguity on the viewer and reveals that paradox is the accurate form of truth.

The arts and sciences seem to be moving in opposite directions. The danger of this is that the sciences do not seem to appreciate the arts. The primary reason for this is that the sciences want to clarify life and simplify it down to its most common denominator as well as concentrate on cause and effect relationships. Generally the arts are interested in none of that. The arts want to muddy the water and introduce ambiguity. They want to say that there are fewer differences between you and me than we would like to think. Art sees that there are CAUSES and effects that are so intricate that it is impossible to untangle the mess. Life is a beautiful knot. Art sees truth as two faced with the viewer looking himself in the mirror so that he is subject *and* object, not one or the other. Science is the attempt to make your life easier. Art wants to make your life more complex—flavorfully complex. Great art makes the viewer work for their cookie. It makes the viewer struggle and makes them want to know what this piece of art means. They need to ask: Why is this art? *That* is the only artistic question.

#61

If you open yourself up enough, you are bound to become an artist; that is what an artist is— openness.

The heartbreak of our first love is like a pre-test for becoming an artist. We fall into love with such innocence and when that love cracks, we are left with two choices: never fully invest ourselves in love again or recommit to love, knowing that it is a potential path to pain. Heartbreak offers us that choice. Hopefully, we decide to trust again after some reflection as to what went wrong. We then have the opportunity to open ourselves, less naively and more intentionally, rather than closing ourselves off from love. It is as if adulthood comes with beauty blinders and those real world responsibilities make us miss the simple marvels of our own world. The artist needs this open attitude. To see great things, I have to risk getting dust in my eyes. It is a return to that child like wonder which makes us stop and realize that everything on earth is something that we ought to pick up and gaze at. What is this? How did it come into being? Who made this? What does it do? The answers are irrelevant. The important thing is the yearning for learning. Most schools in industrialized countries have beat the artist out of us and this is why the heartbreak of first love is a good metaphor. We have to find wonder again and when we do—we have become an artist.

#64

If failure is not near, neither is great art.

Most people feel that they have to get as far away from failure as they can. The artist must have the courage to linger there. If their last project escaped failure then they must go even deeper into the cave. The meaning of growth is to expand your boundaries and to try something new. To do something you are not used to is a risk. With risk, there is the possibility of failure—if you want to call it that. Failure means that you tried, but your project didn't turn out the way that it was intended to. "It's awful!" —but, why? What is wrong and where did it stray? You are being called to fail in order to improve yourself. Is it color mixing or a structural flaw that you did not foresee? You are being asked to pay attention to a detail that you did not consider. A 'failure' points the artist to a weakness that can be over come by learning the lesson that is being shown.

#70

Artistic Fallacy: I want to do something unique AND have everybody love it.

One of the hardest parts of being an artist is controlling one's expectations of how one's work will be received. The truth about what will likely happen is very uninspiring. It is likely that your ground-breaking work will not draw much attention and no one will notice its brilliance. That is nothing to fantasize about and maybe that is why many artists are propelled to work with ambitious thoughts of fame, fortune, and glory. Art is organic and it has to grow on you. So many artists are dead before their work is appreciated and even great work can be met with tepid interest. Apparently when the first impressionistic works came out, a famous art critic said that the group show was done by a bunch of "wild beasts." At least it got some attention at the time. If you are making unique work, don't plan on even getting that. The point is that you have to commit to your project and to some extent be comfortable with the fact that unique is what you are going for. If your poetry is so esoteric that no one can relate to it, then it is going to be difficult for it to become popular. It is like the stuck-up beauty witch from high school. You are always thinking, "wouldn't it be cool if she was just as pretty but NICER!" It just doesn't happen that way. Now, to get everybody to love something, you usually have to make a lot of compromises, avoid anything dark, and chop off your ear.

#74

You can fail as an artist but you can never be a *failure* as an artist.

I think that if you got a printout at the end of your life that listed the number of hours you spent watching TV versus the number of hours you spent creating art, you would be proud if the art hours were higher. This does not mean that your work is going to end up in the Louvre rather than the landfill. The point is, you brought art into being; you added to an understanding of beauty or produced a "message" that needed to be expressed from your deeper insides. You took the project from concept to completion. This is a remarkable process. You probably knew that there would be little fan fare as well. There is no way you are a failure—who else can work under such conditions? No one. Artists are soul producers. Sports are fun because once you understand the simple rules, you can follow the game, root for your team, be proud when they do well, and gripe when they don't. Sports are compelling because they are simple. Coming up with an art project is not. I have heard some artists sit in front of blank canvas until they see a painting appear to them. That is tough! No simple rules, no compelling story line. Notice what happens when you ask someone to "say something" in a foreign language. First of all, they can't do it. Then they produce the most banal phrase. Art is difficult but if you make art you have made the world more beautiful and thus you are a success!

Chapter 7
Singing Elaborations

#1

The intentions of the song must be in the intonations of the singer.

The singer has to find the emotional match for the lyrics or melody in the intonation of his or her voice. Singing is ultimately about emotions and that is why music "takes us places" emotionally and why certain songs strike us when we are in particular moods. The vocal artist thus should consider the various emotional twists of a particular song and try to use one's voice in order to elicit those emotions in the listener. Of course, there are exceptions to this thought particularly if you are performing a comedy where a mismatch between emotional tone and lyrical tone is more appropriate. Morrissey of the *Smiths* effectively mismatched his very somber lyrics with upbeat music (e.g., girlfriend in a coma) to produce a sardonic effect. The key here is that this was an intentional mismatch. When tragic lyrics are accompanied by a tragic voice; generally, you have a moving song.

#10

Singing is a physical event, just like sports, you better practice and you should warm up before the show!

General Thoughts: In learning a new song, one might want to plan their breaths deliberately marking them out with the words on the page. Warming up is also essential for the novice who must get the vocal chords and sinuses clear. The setting must make one comfortable. If performing, always check the sound in an amplified/acoustic environment—which can greatly effect how the singer hears oneself. Like any sport, water intake must range in between dehydration and belching. Obviously, bawdy songs might be best produced under bawdy conditions. This is why some bands have wonderful 'live' albums as well as less than spectacular studio ones.

#11

The beats of a song are the rocks in the river that the vocal waters need to flow over.

When singing the lyrics of a song, the singer can't be too conscientious of the music. The music, like water, must flow through the singer who adds their voice to the mix like a leaf floating upon the water as it goes over rocks, which are the beats of the music. Artistry occurs because the leaf is sometimes ahead and sometimes behind the natural drag of the water. One must know the song and the lyrics so well as to forget the need to remember. It flows forth from the heart (and not the mind). Music is about emotion and never about anything else. The artist is the extreme feeler.

#13

You know when you've got the essence of the song when your own hair stands up while you're singing.

We believe that to evaluate sound it must be listened to; this is only partially correct. Sound must be listened to. But the singer should also pay attention to the rest of the body. If your singing is moving you, it is likely moving others. Singing is a spiritual act and it is done best if it is felt somewhere in addition to the ears. Knowing that you are hitting the right notes is something that you will feel somewhere else. Where is that for you? It is important to know the sacred sign that you get when you are ringing the bell. For me, it is back of the neck goose bumps—some times called aesthetic chills. This means that sound is vibration that you can listen to and also vibrate with.

#15

I can't find my default voice yet, which in the long run might be good because I am attempting to gain control over a number of different voicings.

When searching for a voice, one should listen for a default voice. What I fight with now seems to be other voices within me trying to come out. What I want is a voice that I can start with when exploring a new song, which will allow me to find my way into that song. Certainly, one has "multiple" personalities and multiple voices that are all fighting for airtime. There is a country voice, an opera voice, a punk voice, and others that are trying to influence the voicing of each song. When we are trying to find "our" voice or find our way through a song, we are pruning back the variety of voices to find the right voice for "this" song. My feeling is that when the vocalist finds their voice and they hold that sacred, then they allow that voice to be bent into the musical genre. If you try to let the voices emerge from within you without picking a certain one, you will have trouble controlling the song.

#21

I have the first line to a 1000 different songs.

Each artist gets paid differently in inspiration. I get a lot of little seeds that need to be nurtured in order to grow into something larger. The maxims in this book are my fruit. I get the beginnings of songs and poems from these little seeds, but I still need to work on them. The most difficult work of art is deciding: what is my next project and whether or not I see promise in the work. Most of the time, I don't make very systematic decisions. I don't do "series" or even know what my next piece will be. This means that with songs, I only write one at a time and only if it really strikes me. I don't recommend this approach to you. It works for me because I am writing and painting and playing music and I have to go with what calls me! That sometimes means I put the guitar down for months on end. I just need a break from that particular medium. I do accumulate the song's first lines and record the melody on a recorder even during those breaks. I try to preserve the essence of the song so that I can revisit it, should I choose to, at another date. I probably won't. What both art and nature teach us is that if you drop a lot of seeds, some will grow and others won't. Sometimes other artistic creatures can pick up your seeds and find them nourishing!

#27

It's not that you don't know how to sing. It's that you don't know which voice to sing in.

It seems to me that to sing well, one has to pick songs that one feels emotionally connected to and songs that fit oneself vocally. Oftentimes when singing, we find ourselves at a mismatch with both. The song sounds flat and we cannot find "our voice." In these cases, we start singing in one voice and then only find a groove at a certain point in the song. These are the two competing voices. The voice that we find in the strong groove then has to be followed, uncovered and nurtured. Each step of the way, there are opportunities to tingle and tease the listener. We must backtrack and discover those spots. We have to try and harness the strong voice in order to reclaim this voice in spots where the weaker voice reigns. The powerful song grabs us early and takes us on a ride and finding the voice that allows one to let it out is the hard work of singing. Sing songs that make you feel the tingle.

30

Teach yourself to sing in cursive!

The singer must find the confidence to experiment with their voice and must also find the freedom from self-consciousness in order to roll the words in the way that they wish so that some additional flare can be created. When we learn how to write, just as when we learn to sing, there is a certain mechanical quality in doing the act. With letters, we are told to stay within the lines, to replicate exactly what the instructor does, and, of course, we are rewarded for good penmanship. I remember sitting in study hall and watching girls write their names over and over attempting to give some style to their signature. One may do the same thing with their voice. The singer can practice singing the words in ways that can occasionally give the listener a twist. If we think about our favorite song and the part of that song that we like the best, inevitably we are given something that we did not expect.

#42

I find that when I'm writing a song, there are often two songs that are competing to get out at one time. One has to allow both to be born.

People have likened creativity to pregnancy throughout history. I have found that, occasionally, in song writing there are twins! The artist becomes confused since one is imagining that there is only a single child coming. However, the melody or lyrical content wants to separate itself into two different directions, and if we are able to be patient with what is emerging, it is possible that we can allow these fraternal twins to come out and be different souls. The method that has helped me the most is to find the melody that is embedded in the words. Then I can sing to myself in a stream of consciousness fashion. I almost don't know I'm making a song until I find myself amused by the lyrics. Next, I begin turning the couplet into a stanza. Along the way the melody can advance itself. New stanzas are created by letting the rhyme and the melody pull the words out of your mouth. Do not worry if the words make sense. Let them flow (and record them—if you can). The melody itself can develop some complexity with repeated practice. Very often there is more music in the song than you initially believe. This can be teased out by imagining that you are playing the part of the melody using different instruments. Often, I will actually get two songs that have quite different vocal beginnings.

#43

A song is a piece of architecture.

Each song requires its own time—a development period. One must be patient and discover the voice that the song calls for. One must discover the rhythms in the song that groove best with the singer and the guitarist. This often means choosing from a variety of emerging possibilities and a variety of paths. It is like life itself—some people grow up quick; some are old before their time; others are youthful into their late years.

The frustration occurs when there are multiple voices emerging or multiple riffs developing, and yet, no preferred form jells; one might feel frustrated, but you are closer now than you might imagine. The proper form will emerge. The goal is to capture all that is there. You might have various parts to the same song or various songs. I am surprised how many songs you can write in the same key with largely the same chord progression. The songs will be unique because the slightest alterations take you on a remarkably different journey.

#53

To sing, my soul needs to vibrate.

As a songwriter, I find that the words and music are relatively easy to produce after one finds the original verse or chorus. The problem that I encounter is giving life to those words while singing. Singing is truly about "inspiration" breathing life into the song. Self-consciousness is primarily the enemy of singing. Self-consciousness keeps the singing system tight and prevents the fullness of the soul from reverberating through the song. Knowing this and being able to do something about it are two different things.

Again, this is not a cognitive task. Like so much of art, it is about the heart. Apparently, there is a certain amount of self-debugging that is needed. Singing might be the most psychological of the arts because anxiety must be confronted and a sense of confidence can only come through quality, practice, and chasing the emotion of the song. Maybe a little mantra will also help: Be Free, Be Free, Be Free. Practice with purpose, know you are worthy and Be Free. Freedom in performance is beauty.

#60

I need to sing in the car, in the shower, in the woods—anywhere I am free—sing among freedom until you can be free amongst others.

Singing in public can be a bad idea if you are not ready for it. There are other art forms that allow you to do your work in which, once it is finished, you can then bring it to the eyes of others. Singing requires practice, but the show requires you to do your work in the presence of people. Self-consciousness is not a helpful item in a singer's toolbox. Practice has to be done in places where the singer is free to obtain the least amount of self-consciousness as possible. It is alternatively helpful to adopt an "I don't give a fuck attitude" toward anyone's judgment. A lot of great lead vocalists have had such an attitude.   It is sexy and dangerous—but problematic for your non-professional life! Clearly, there is no "I" in singing. The singer has to become the song, become the music, become the message, and become the emotion. Freedom means letting go of the 'ego.' In doing so, all that exists is "presence." Freedom is confidence. A painter can be at one's own opening in an almost anonymous fashion whereas the singer is the focal point of the event.

#64

You have to get to the heart of the song even if you have to hide from it at first.

Two good questions about any song you are going to play or sing are: a) what is the emotional heart of the song? and b) where is the penultimate moment? Feeling the emotional heart is often not as simple as it seems. We often speak of music in terms of two emotions: happy and/or sad songs. The successful singer is someone who takes us on a kind of 'sacred' journey. The voice has to reflect some sort of emotional change throughout the song. Even if it is a "sad" song, we have to fluctuate it so that the song's emotions bottom out somewhere. So the song should be addressed as sad AND what else: apathetic, hopeful, bitter, violent, funny? The more that one can tease out the emotional possibilities of a song, the more the song will seem like a ride. Sacred means feeling many emotions at once. The sacred is always difficult to put into words because it is overflowing with multiple emotions. The climax is where the song 'bottoms out' or hits its apex. Most songs have it near the end but not at the very end. Some song craft might hold back a portion of the power and then let it all out. If you are writing the song's lyrics, you might also consider where the strongest stanzas are and how they relate to the emotional climax of the song. If you get this all lined up and properly orchestrated then you will have a powerful song. Everything is there for the reason that the artist has intended.

#69

Music is universal because music is an emotional regulator.

Music is found in every human society that has ever existed. Language is there for communication purposes and it makes sense that every culture needs language for practical purposes. Because of this, it might be easy to assume that music is there for "entertainment" purposes, yet that seems to be a superficial understanding of what music does. Music helps us feel. Feeling is what we need to do in order to be human. Oddly, we have been told that we need to "think" in order to be human. Descartes' statement, "I think therefore I am" puts thinking at the center of the western world. This is a shame. Thinking without feeling is a formula for disaster and that is what the 20th century showed us. Thinking is a divider. We have smart, smarter, and genius. It is inheritably elitist. Music is emotional. It is a uniter. It makes us want to dance—together. It makes us want to sing—together. When we sing the simple songs, we are a community. There are no differences. We belong. Great music "stirs" us and takes us to emotional places that it wants to: We are just passengers. Music takes us out of our power position as "destiny directors" and puts us back as observers of the sometimes beautiful and sometimes cruel results of this tumultuous universe. Your song is the vibration that you sing.

#74

Dreams make good song plots.

Articulating the actions that happen in your night dreams is helpful to the artist in a number of ways. First, by writing out or telling someone your dreams, you are automatically practicing a kind of art form. Dreams are frequently more visual than oral, so the task of translating the images into words is kind of a poetic task and usually it is not an easy one. Most of the time we have a tendency to report the dream like a newspaper person; just the "facts" so we stick to the plot of the dream. It is sometimes fun to try and tell the plot of the dream in a poem form with a rhyme scheme. I have had good success writing songs this way. Very little had to be constructed that wasn't already there. Dreams also have a tendency to be interesting and symbolic. Anything you write with flair should also contain those same qualities. I believe that one of the most important things a person can do for their creativity is to keep track of their dreams and write them down. Try to write a dream out in a rhyme scheme and you have a song.

#80

Singing is an act of courage.

Several times I had to resist writing a disclaimer for this chapter. I feel that I have enough skill in the topics of the other chapters so that something can be gained from my insights. I cannot fully feel that about my singing and music skills. I have not been able to feel confident enough in my skills or comfortable enough with my tools to make a significant contribution to music. I have played out a few times but did not feel free. So much of this chapter has been the conveying of my own struggles and the challenge of trying to be at home with my voice. I have not gotten there as of the publication of this book. I do feel that I don't know if what I am saying here is relevant to people who are singing, but since I do feel that some of my observations in other areas are helpful, at least some of these might also be helpful to the beginner. I will leave it to the reader to make that decision. I do believe that singing is an act of courage. You are baring your soul to others. Your voice can reveal emotions and make others feel pain or passion. A song is a mental state that you are sharing with the world. When they love your song, you have introduced a new perspective to the world. Singing is freedom at its highest level.

Chapter 8
Painting Elaborations

#3

Work on something long enough until you find a limit in it.

I have never been an artist who likes to take on the same subject matter in the same way. There have been many artists who do such a thing. This may be a way to have others recognize your work immediately, but it also carries the possibility of stagnation. I am a firm believer that one must try to avoid formulas and attempt to challenge one's self through your chosen medium(s). It is easy to say, "Don't mess with success" but the artist can't become a machine or a caricature of one's self. The best way, I have found, to avoid this is to try to push the medium that one is working on to its limits. If one is working with a particular paper or surface, the next project should continue toward getting the maximum effect out of that product. If a person has a successful design, the next version should be an elaboration of it, not a replication. The work of art should leave you with a question, an idea or a problem that you can work on in your next painting.

#6

I don't like my beauty sweet!

Everyone has there own tastes concerning art. Becoming an artist means to refine your own tastes. This means to become more sensitive to what you are sensitive to, or as Nietzsche says, "Become who you are." This means that you ought to find what you like and really try to understand what it is that draws you into another person's artwork. When I say that I don't like my beauty sweet, I am saying that I don't like art to be too pretty. I have to have some sour or some darkness in there. Why? Because I don't see life as always being happy, joyful, and innocent. Most of the beauty that I see comes out of the shadow side, the deterioration of things. If I had to photograph a brand new car versus those Cuban cars from the 1950s, I'd choose the Cubans. I see perfect beauty as intensely false, sort of like these photo-shopped models that are artificially made "more" beautiful and even impossibly beautiful. There is a sort of fantasy or naivety in the beauty that is not for my tastes, despite the fact that I have made nude paintings. Lighthearted, happy go lucky art is not my thing (right now). I think we can always add that "right now," since I might decide to change and go through a happy period at some point. For now, I avoid sweets and I know why. This should help me to find the art that I want to make and challenge me to make art that is more 'me.'

#11

Some things will never achieve stability until you tighten the final screw.

You must have faith in yourself and your project if you are going to do challenging work. As I have often needed help from time to time while constructing a sculpture, I have been amazed at how my helpers have informed me that the project "won't work," "it won't stand up," or "it just can't be made." I'm always puzzled by these statements since they come from folks who have seen me do other projects that did work. Creativity doesn't mean that you have all the answers at the beginning—it means that you can problem solve when a problem appears. If something doesn't work, the artist can ask, "Why is this not doing what I want it too?" or "Why doesn't this look right?" It is not a matter of planning ahead for everything but addressing the problems as they reveal themselves. Inspiration gives us a vague blue print for a project rather than a foolproof instruction booklet. We may have to loosen some screws that were tight before and bring them back down evenly. But if it doesn't stand, then put another screw in it. Every art requires the ability to improvise.

#14

You need to know color so you can forget about color! The painter must learn, practice, and

explore with such regularity that eventually what took reflection is now replaced with intuition.

I want to choose my colors like I choose my clothes in the morning. Just reach in there, grab the one you want and move on with the day. I dislike it when I have to hem and haw about the right color. In other words, I have a lot to learn about color choice right now. Heck, I haven't even had a "period" yet where I just go out and buy a bunch of funky colors and then paint everything backwards. It's not that you can't get a lot of expression out of black and white or the standard colors. I just don't feel like I have "mastered" color; in fact, I feel like I don't know what I'm doing. That doesn't mean that I haven't made some good paintings but it does mean that I have a ways to go in my growth as an artist. You know you are good at something when you don't think.

#23

Let the mind fill it in!

A lot of the paintings that I create have an element of chaos to them. There are some random splotches and suggestive blends of paint. Sometimes, though, I try to add to areas where I think there is a need for an additional paint blob. The funny thing is that it is quite difficult to make a non-random piece of paint look random. If you are working on big picture stuff with a lot of negative space, then maybe you are better served by moving on and letting the viewer's mind fill in the missing details. A painting can be fun because you can barely tell what it is, but then, when you do see it, it is impossible not to see it. If you are not doing detail pieces then don't get slowed down by adding detail to an otherwise detail-less piece. If you are going for 'expressive' work then sometimes more details "spell" it out too much. The real beauty of the Rorschach Ink Blot is that it allows the viewer to participate in the process by allowing their mind to place the form on the material.

#33

Painting is a lot more thoughtful than one might think.

Painting is not always a relaxing situation. One is constantly faced with choices, decisions, and doubts. Some aspect of the painting is "not quite right" or it somehow is "not bold enough." Hours are often spent staring at the same spot. What is wrong here? No answer. The artist puts that piece aside. Months may pass. Every couple of months, the painting will get a few moments of review but the work mostly gains disgust in the mind of the artist. Sometimes the work is never finished. Occasionally a second "eureka" moment leads to a solution. Recently, I pulled a framed painting of mine off the wall because I noticed an area that needed some more pizzazz. A few paintings can occupy all of the "back burners" in one's mind.

#36

Can you work hard enough to finish those pieces that are weak? Their weakness is the spot of greatest opportunity.

There have been a few times when the drive to finish a painting has begun to fizzle. My loss of enthusiasm almost always coincides with the mismatch between what I had imagined and the piece that appears before me. Here is where the real artistic battle begins. I have had paintings that I just forget about for several months and even years. When I do re-discover them, I often get a minor glimpse at what had drawn me to the project in the first place, but often no idea at a solution. This is the pregnancy of the piece that I have referred to in other places. Something passionate, daring, or "radical" needs to emerge from this layoff. Often the mismatch between the imagined and the real is that the imagined was powerful, stunning, or colorful and the real does not strike the creator in that way. What needs to be done then? Part of it is to overcome our own habits of painting in order to allow one's self the freedom to paint with "reckless abandon." We are asking for permission to be more different than we have previously been.

#48

Sometimes it is best to leave a spontaneous painting alone. Even a little touching up can take away from the most profound accidents.

There is a certain amount of chaos that all paintings need to have. Sometimes this comes in the form of an accident: a drip, a smear, too much paint here, the wrong color there, etc. Frequently, our initial response is to see this as a mistake; however, if we can resist the urge to make an immediate correction—which, coincidently, often makes the situation worse—we come to appreciate the "flaw." It adds a sense of freshness to the work. It reminds us that nothing here on earth is flawless. Soon, the more we look at the painting, the more we enjoy the flaw. When we finish the work, we may even tell another viewer that it is our favorite part of the painting. This holds true for sketches as well. After looking at a quick drawn sketch, there is often the desire to add more detail, but sometimes even just a few more marks can transform the sketch's simplistic beauty into something contrived in its detail. Removing paint (from a painting) is harder than not adding it in the first place.

#52

Floundering is a part of art.

No one can produce masterpiece after masterpiece, which is probably a good thing. There is something to be said about being frustrated with your art. Asking yourself why you can't do on the page what you want to do is likely to make you a better artist in the long run. The odds are, you have run into the limits of your artistic skills. Some new type of practice is now necessary for you to grow. Now comes the floundering. Even success requires that you reinvent yourself; otherwise you become an artistic caricature of yourself. One must take what one has gained from experience. Add that to one's intuition so that one is able to both be patient during gestation but also be able to choose projects that extend their range as an artist as one continues to take appropriate creative risks.

#54

A failed painting doesn't mean you should quit, but you *should* be more radical.

When I think that I am finished with a painting but still feel dissatisfied with it, it is most often because I did not take enough chances with that painting. In each work, there has to be some kind of challenge for both the artist and the viewer. This might mean choosing an unusual color or color scheme for ordinary objects, or in some other way destabilizing the viewer's reception of the piece. One of the small but mighty rewards of being an artist is when one sees a patron cruising past various pieces of art in order to "see the whole show" and then the patron suddenly comes to a screeching halt in front of your piece. To elicit that response, the artist is going to have to take chances. The piece needs pop. When I look at my work I never like to think 'Oh that's nice." To me, nice is a failure. I want to disrupt the *gallery shuffle* and in order to do that something has to stick out. Luckily, it can be the message, style, color, or degree of difficulty, etc. Until your vision does something, your painting does nothing.

#60

You always paint against yourself.

It is hard to figure out how we artists get anything done. Sometimes I find myself inspired to come out and work, but when I get there I see that I forgot to clean up my workspace from the night before. Once I get that done, I have a little less of that inspiration. I usually still get some work done, but if I could do a better job here and there I could hit some of these moments with a little momentum. I've had other incidents where I have been out of the only paint that I needed. These are small errors that have the ability to ruin moods. We cannot necessarily change our personality. I get certain benefits from being a free wheeling artist. I get all kinds of transmissions on art, poetry, and music. If I want to be highly organized, I'm sure I will find that difficult and it will also take away some of the good. *Painting against yourself* means trying to get away from practices that hinder your painting and your artistic process. I don't think you can ever clean them out completely, but if you could gain some control, I'd like to think that this phase would be "the most productive period of his career." I can't imagine that it could last forever. Maybe I could make a list "What I can live without" and "What I can live with." One thing a painter can live without —not having any paint.

#65

If you don't like the painting it is not done.

Well, despite saying, "Let the mind fill it in," artists also should use their own judgment about when a piece of work is finished. If you look at it from various distances and determine that the piece doesn't look right—then it is not finished. Sometimes it is best to put the piece away for a while, like a couple of months and come back to it. Lots of things happen to people in a couple of months, especially now that we can see thousands of artistic images a week on the internet. Maybe in that time frame something that you saw will give you the insight to solve the "what's wrong with this picture?" Maybe something that you learn in doing your next painting will be helpful to you finishing the previous one. Don't rush a project just to finish it. When you feel that you can live with this piece of art being associated with you, kind of like "this is one of my children," then sign it.

#71

How do you know it is done? When the odds are that your addition could just as much end up as a distraction. That is when you sign the piece.

This is my method. An artist gets to the point where there is only one part of the painting that is of serious consideration. Then the decision starts revolving around the question: Should I try to "fix" this to my liking? At that moment when you say to yourself: "If I try to adjust this I could really mess it up." "It might take me a long time (whatever that would be for you) to bring it back around." This is the time to sign the piece and set down the brush. Very rarely have I ever questioned a signed piece, although like any creator, I have noticed something that I did not like in a completed work. Now, the odds that the viewer would automatically hawk to that detail, is extremely unlikely. As we know from talking to anyone about a piece of work, art is intensely personal and most people do not express the identical feelings that the artist was trying to capture. That's what is so cool about art: It means more than it was intended to mean.

#73

Every error is the opportunity to improvise.

I have a little chaos in every painting; so, almost always there is something that goes on that is beyond my control. In each of those cases, the artist is presented the chance to 'think on her feet" and try to figure out how to convert the ill placed paint into some kind of form or figure that now fits into the painting. I have a number of tools handy that I can use to scrape, scratch, carve, or smooth the paint into something else. Often, by necessity, I have to make quick judgments and change the original plan. It is kind of like a partnership with the work. It wants to be something a little different from what I planned. I have to let it have some input, don't I?

Anything that is born wants a little say in what it becomes. I think it is even better than the ladies who weave an error into their project so they don't have to worry about making a prefect tapestry. Here, the painting is exerting its will. We may call it a "happy accident" but I like to think of it as collaboration. There's a little bit of destiny in every work of art!

#81

New Motto: Do it! Screw it! Fix it!

This is going to be my approach for a while. "Do it!" means that when you get an idea, don't wait too long before you start it. Get something initially on paper. Get the piece started. It will look okay, but you will need to improve it somehow. "Screw it!" means that if you attempt to "improve" work, you will actually screw it up more. What has happened is that you began with a stream of consciousness and while this is promising, it becomes 'incoherent' in parts. You recognize the individualistic or idiosyncratic nature of the piece and realize that no one other than you (and sometimes not even you) could follow this train of thought. So, you have to add structure to it in order to make the piece coherent. This structure does not seem to fit well on top of the stream of consciousness part (or vice versa). That is why these two attitudes together appear as a screw up; but it is not a screw up because you are an artist and you can solve the problem. The "Fix it!" is a reconciliation of the first two parts. A synchronizing of the artist's skills is to make the two parts flow into each other so that the inspiration and the execution form a unity. Ultimately, there are no mistakes in art, just opportunities.

Chapter 9
Poetry Elaborations

#1

What makes language a poem is the deliberate beauty of each word in context.

I am surprised at just how many words can actually be removed from a poem without that poem losing the original meaning. Scholars realize this, too, when they have to write an abstract of 120 words only to find themselves writing 20 words over the limit. Moreover, poets can get caught up in the placement of words, where their position does not affect the meaning, but instead affects the rhythm of the line. A poet can spend a half hour debating on whether or not to say, "We were both unscathed" versus "We both were unscathed." The difference between writing and poeting is that every word must have a purpose. The words that do not have a purpose get in the way. Everything is scrutinized by the poet. It must be there for a reason or else it is fat. Poetry is the ultimate in intentionality.

#10

Poems are not really meant to be experienced auditorially but rather in the flesh. I want to feel your poems on the back of my neck.

I have tried to understand what is meant by "spiritual" over the last several years since this term has become more in vogue. I am left with the impression that I have had a spiritual experience when I have been *touched*. This seems to be the moments that I have felt the deepest emotions a human can feel. In those cases I have frequently gotten those goose bumps for non-frigid reasons; they are mostly moments of epiphany, holiness, spirit, and profound emotion. This is my spiritual sign: Goose bumps mean that I am feeling the spiritual in my flesh. You might have other signs, but it is wise to know what they are. Perhaps music can most easily evoke this experience, but we might also feel it when we see great beauty, when we are in the presence of a compassionate act, or when we hear some form of genuine speech. And what is poetry? Is it genuine speech that hopes to elicit a great cathartic emotion? Isn't that why we write it? We don't want dead words. We don't want to be so obscure that the reader feels any further alienation. We want community. When you and I become we, we might finally become free.

#12

Having a life poem—versus not having one—will determine whether a nice bottle of wine turns into a beautiful one.

Every once in a while, we will meet a person who can recite a poem by heart in its entirety. What a beautiful practice that a person has taken the time to memorize something because she has found it to be so meaningful. It seems to me that most of us know only a couple of lines of poetry or the chorus to a number of songs. But wouldn't it be worth investing the time to practice a particular meaningful poem and commit it to memory? Shouldn't we all have a life poem? Isn't a poem that you know by heart like a prayer? You are choosing to know the work personally, choosing to embed it into your soul, and choosing to have it with you whenever you choose to recite it. This life poem is yours to share and I'm sure you will find that there are more opportunities to share it than you might have imagined. This is a key ingredient in making a special life: sharing great art. By cherishing a life poem we add color to our character and make our life more like a work of art.

#15

Pain without meaning is trauma. Poetry makes pain meaningful.

Poetry acts as a forming agent for emotions and helps shape our experiences that were so obscure in our past. We can often get stuck in the past because we experience troubles that we cannot transcend. We have heard about people who were "never the same" after some particular tragedy. The poet works on articulating these obscure feelings by placing experiences into words and giving the troubles some form of meaning. Meaning allows experience to be contained, observed, and incorporated because now it is given some sense—even if the event initially seemed senseless. That is why poetry is emotional and symbolic. It is not the language of the actual: facts and figures-who, what, where, when, and how. Poetry is the language of meaning and meaning is always more than fact; it is figurative, deep and touching. When pain has meaning, there was a purpose to that pain and thus the pain was a lesson that was revealed by the poetic. Trauma is senseless pain. Poetry is the transformation of trauma into meaning.

#22

The truth is found between the first and second draft. You never say what you think you say when you first say it.

It amazes me how much ideas will resist being put into words. Even when talking, we find it difficult to describe experiences, explain feelings, and express our thoughts in ways that feel complete to us. All first attempts at writing about a subject can at best be considered sketches. Anyone who takes the time to write down a dream is confronted with placing images into verbal elements. Attempts to capture these dreams are often greatly inadequate. They may capture the plot but can never grasp the richness and details of the dream. I am often surprised to find how many pages of writing it takes to write what initially seemed like quite a simple dream. So many details have to be left out. All the ideas that appear so clear in our mind are actually very difficult to articulate. Almost every time I re-read something I have just written, I think, "That is not quite what I meant" or "That's not what I meant at all." I can comprehend the claim that language is an inadequate tool to express experience; however, this is probably not true because the poet is able to craft language in a way that makes experience seem more meaningful. The main difference is that the poet never submits a first draft.

#30

An author's greatest achievement is not that the reader understands her intentions but that the reader is sparked to thoughts of his own.

Part of our intellectual development requires that we come to understand how we best think and what our processes are which lead us to our most bountiful thoughts. Oftentimes, when we are struggling to get through a text, we see ourselves as losing focus because our reading is interrupted by our wandering thoughts. Sometimes with frustration we will ask ourselves to "concentrate" and be frustrated by our inability to move thorough the test with pace. Instead of frustration, I suggest we should be pleased that text is sparking our own interest or confusion. It seems to me that the text is asking us to be processed and this lack of focus is actually our own thought. This "own" thought is undervalued because it takes our mind away from the author's intentions. But if we can permit ourselves some folly, we might find that the author's greatest achievement is not his or her own words but the thoughts that the reader comes to by way of analogy. I measure the greatness of the book by how much I have written in the margins.

#35

The reason for writing down a thought is to free your mind for the next one (instead of concentrating on remembering the last one).

I am an avid dream recorder and try my best to write down my dreams immediately in the morning. Obviously, I can't always do that. I have noticed that if I have had a dream that I, somehow, was not able to write down, I often do not get a new dream for a couple of days. Once I write that dream down, I am often immediately rewarded with one or two more dreams. I also believe this to be true of these little maxims that run through my mind. If I stumble across one that I like and I don't have a pen or paper, I really have to struggle in order to remember it. During the time I am trying to remember the thought, I certainly have no new transmissions mainly because I am saying the line over and over in my head trying to memorize it. If you don't record the line on paper, it acts more like a dream that will disappear and cannot be traced back at all. Sometimes, I find myself straining to try to remember a line that I thought I would not forget. Other times I have at thought at night and do not want to fully wake up to record it. This is always heartbreaking much so like a fish that slips off a hook. This happens way too much. Take the time to grab the line—take your transmissions.

#36

Every word is a junkyard.

The fun part of poetry is discovering the versatility of each word. We all know that a word has several meanings and any particular meaning is determined by the context and intention of the writer and the reader. But words inherently drag with them other meanings that the poet enjoys playing with. The sound of the word also has a multiplicity of potential rhymes and off rhymes. They often leave the listener feeling a sense of amazement that the poet could choose to rhyme "shoe" and "good" and apparently manipulate the situation so that this works both rhythmically and semantically. Two words can stand next to each other and seem like such a contrast that the odd bedfellows give us a sense of joy and irony. The meaning of a word in and of itself can change and even evolve into its opposite. A word can simultaneously be an insult and a compliment. In short, a word is a junkyard that contains pieces of meaning from the past along with new meanings, new uses, and new configurations from the present that can always be made from its remnants.

#40

You don't set out to be a poet; you earn the right to be one. You end up a poet because you've been blown open by the explosive perspective of words.

It is hard to say exactly what you mean because you don't know what you feel at the most important minutes of your life. Speaking about these times is an attempt to structure experience and often times we either reach for the wrong word or the words are too elusive. In addition, words never have one meaning and can be seen as loose tools or skeleton keys that open various doors in the mind of our listeners; listeners who have a variety of locks in their own minds. The person who becomes a poet is a person who wants to open the sentence to various levels of meaning. The poet wants the words to have multiple doors. You can make the sentence work one way or the other but hopefully you will be able to see it both ways. The poet uses the expansive qualities to spread points of beauty and meaning. All great art has multiple levels of understandability.

#45

Reading, Writing, and Reflection are the three paths to improving one's mind. If you want to sharpen your mind you have to rub it against something abrasive.

I find it fascinating that in the great art eras of the past, the artists would often be reading the most up to date philosophy and sometimes physics as well! Their art attempted to express visually or poetically the trends in their culture's thought. It is like one's mind, both artistically and intellectually, needs to be sharpened. And one proven way to do this is to read difficult things like philosophy and physics. The artist, who is seeking insights and ideas for their artwork, might delve into other disciplines as a "spark" to get the wheels in their mind moving. Moreover, one's grasping for understanding may not lead to understanding, but it often leads to thought generation in the forms of hypotheses, analogies, and metaphors. I frequently write in the margins of my books what I think the author is trying to say. I compare this work with other thinkers that I am more familiar with, and sometimes I compare it to songs or artwork that I know. This is reflection on the work. Notice that it doesn't matter if I am "right." It is thinking and thinking is hindered by the need for 'correctness.'

#49

A made metaphor means a new species has moved into our language gene pool.

At the end of the year, news-programs often recount those things that disappeared or appeared that year. It is always fun to see the lists of new words that entered the vernacular. We can have some appreciation for what the new word opens for us. A word is a code or short hand for something bigger. And that word is a new piece of our language puzzle, a new tool to play with, and a new opening to walk into. Metaphors are the same way. They allow us to understand our world in a meaningful package that reveals a concise analogy. Over time, metaphors become cliché and overused because they are a way to simplify complex thoughts in a relatively short phrase. Sometimes people will botch the metaphor that actually makes us take a second look at the original intention. Yogi Berra was great at this—saying things like "It's not over until it's over." The poet tries to avoid the old metaphors and attempts to create new ones that at minimum show a fresh take on something even if it is not brand spanking new. Metaphors are the air freshener of language!

#50

Who needs toys when you have language to play with?

To play with language is a simple joy. All it takes is a playful attitude. I remember being a freshmen in college and meeting a bunch of people for the first time. I was struck by how habitual our language patterns were. Everyone asked the same questions, "Where are you from?" or "What's your major?" I found it disheartening that as intelligent people we are basically so robotic with our talk. I decided that I was going to answer all standard questions in unusual ways. Just to be difficult. That was the beginning of something much larger; I wanted to use language to be an interesting person and maybe more importantly I wanted to be involved in interesting conversations. It turns out that the only way to do so is to break the habit of talking in an ordinary way. So I would give non-traditional answers to ordinary questions. For example, when someone would ask me "How are you today?" instead of saying "good" or "fine" I would answer, "I'm special!" You can tell a lot about your conversation partner by how they respond to your slightly off response: Someone who says "Okay, whatever" is someone to let move on. You know they want the status quo. Someone who says, "That's good, I like that!" is someone who you might want to chat with. Language is the ultimate toy because you can go somewhere that you never expected to go from starting at such a standard opening.

#53

The mind of the poet was meant to wander.

I love having conversations with people that take left turns. It is fun to share stories when your story can remind someone of one of their stories and their story can lead you to another of your own. At some point you ask yourself, "How did we start talking about this when we began by talking about that?" Your conversation got there because you let it wander. It can be followed backwards if need be, but wandering is a helpful practice. You can also do this on your own. This is sometimes best accomplished in solitude—a place where most of the good poetry is made. All you have to do is say, "Let's just let my thoughts do whatever they want to today." I grant myself the freedom to entertain whatever comes my way. If this thought looks interesting, I'll pick it up. If I'm not in the mood for that right now then I can pick up a thought from yesterday. One problem with our highly scheduled lives is that there is rarely any down time. It is go, go, go! When we take the time to reflect or watch people or let our thoughts wander, we often benefit later on; thus, in no way are we 'wasting' time. When I'm writing songs, I just let whatever comes out of my mouth be the song. There are a lot of nothings that come out this way. But after about five minutes of nothing, I will usually put together a good stanza. Let it flow and capture what is worthy. You can edit out the bad later and continue to add stanzas once the story line becomes more defined.

#59

Bandaged with words: Poetry has healing powers because it encapsulates the emotional shrapnel and gives it form.

All forms of art seem to be intent on expressing some deep observation. Acts of poetry are often produced when a pocket of emotional energy is tapped into with words, much like drilling for oil. Similarly, the words often flow with the same exuberance as an oil well when first tapped. Writing poetry is a healing act because many times deep feelings that have been isolated and have remained mute are now given a chance to speak and so they gush! Some event may happen to us that is so bad that we don't want to talk about it and so we ignore it, try not to speak it, and hide from it. This is a bad policy since feelings don't go away and, in fact, grow in the dark. Hurt can only leave if it is shown the light of day and articulated. Speaking about the troubling event gives the experience some form and shape and allows it to be extracted. So poetry and psychotherapy are both intended to hit those dark areas and bring them to the surface so that the person can be freed from what has so long been hidden.

#60

The poet's job is to make the public feel what they miss when they watch the tragedies at six.

The poet is tasked with making the reader feel more. The poet helps the reader feel and see more beauty in the world and thus to connect with a pathos of life. Poetry helps transform the ordinary and overlooked into a fresh revelation. The poet is a pointer who shows the reader that something important has happened. The poet has learned how to maneuver words in order to make feelings appear when thoughts had previously been able to avoid such emotions. The poets take the rational and add the emotional back into our lives. The poet's job is to release meaning that is trapped in the crevices of the person's soul. The poet smelts out the meaning while applying the fricative power of words. Our TV deadens us and we have to be reawakened by the poet. Murder, death, fire, kidnapping are all incidents on the news but they have been stripped of all their tragedy, "…and now for the weather and sports." The poet reminds us that those are persons now gone are not just 'characters' on a reality show of life, but the poet personalizes tragedy and brings meaning to the senseless.

#63

Poetry is finding joy in the ambiguity of language.

The joy of poetry is that you are surprised by what is said. The joy of poetry is that the word appearing in a particular spot opens up a door that you did not know was there. The poet's skill lies in the knowledge of when to counter the reader's expectations; knowing when a train of thought needs to take a left turn and finding an opportunity to imply two different meanings with the use of only one word. Language is world creation and world expansion and the poet is always adding on new rooms. Ambiguity means it could be both. Truth suggests that there is one. But the poet knows that truth is found in paradox and this means that the truth is ambiguous.

#76

The stories that you tell over and over are the poems you are being called to write.

We all find ourselves sharing a story in front of our friends and sometimes in front of a class or audience. Stories that get repeated frequently should start to signal the teller that the narrative account of this event is very significant to one's life. A story repeated is a coat hook moment in life and probably has enough value for you to make the effort to turn that moment into poetry or a short story. In fact, it seems that Western History started out that way with the Iliad and the Odyssey. The storytellers had to commit it to rhyme just so others might be able to remember it for an eternity. For us, it might be autobiography by poems; these are the great events of your life and the things that you have experienced as meaningful. What a beautiful collection this would be for us to read when we are near the end.

Chapter 10
Creativity Elaborations

#7

Just remember that most experimental failures are often seen as "turning points."

When we envision a project, naturally we don't include the trials and tribulations that will actually be required to complete it. We often imagine things going very smoothly. But I ask you to think of a favorite piece of artwork that you have created or even a proud moment in your life. What I believe you will find is that those projects were on the brink of failure if not once, several times. It is frequently under the circumstances of repeated obstacles that creativity is tapped into at its deepest level. True and deep insight often come from working relentlessly on a project, but oddly enough, the "Eureka" moment comes when we are taking a break from our work. The turning point is when we think we have exhausted the possible answers to the question, "how else can I do this?" and then we are surprised that a most obvious—and frequently a quite simple—solution pops into our head. It is only then that we wonder why we did not see this before.

#8

Inspiration is seeing pure possibility.

I understand why it is difficult for artists to be happy with all of their work. Having the inspiration to work artistically often means that one must be visited by powerful visions of *pure possibility*. As one tries to capture that view, there are setbacks, revisions, and even the memory decay of the original idea. Being an artist is much like trying to write down a dream. By the time you find your pen and paper, you have lost at least a third of the dream. All you can say is, "There was more detail to the story but I can't remember it." The same is true of most art forms; sometimes we can only paint the scraps. This must not discourage us because seeing pure possibility is a gift in and of itself and being able to capture some of it is both a calling and a talent.

#12

All creativity is the articulation of something that wants to be seen.

What is coming into being through the artist is something that wants to be born. The artist is the medium through which the project has found the right source for expression. Sometimes people make this process sound too passive as if the artist is some kind of conduit and just waits around to be struck by inspiration. This is not the case at all. To give birth means to go into labor. Even before the human gives birth she is pregnant for many months and the pregnancy changes her physically, behaviorally, and psychologically. Creation is not passive in any way—like pregnancy, it doesn't always look like you are doing something, but you are nourishing the unborn. How does an artist nourish a project or put oneself in the position to receive the artistic insight? First, the artist seeks by appreciating the beauty of the work of others and then by refining her eye. By looking at the work of others, one starts to see what it is that is contained in her vision of beauty. Second, the artist continues to nourish the next project by working on previous projects of her own. Working on one project is consistently the greatest producer of thoughts about future projects. Third, the artist nourishes the next project by interacting with others and listening to their thoughts on art, whether that be reading, writing, reflection, conserving, or listening. Artistic inspiration seems to come through two-part insight. There has to be an opening and something that is seeking light. The artist provides the opening and the project has to see the artist's light as its opportunity to become a seedling. There's a famous quote attributed to the poet Rumi that says, "that which you seek also seeks you."

#17

Creativity is a constructive path to the future.

How can we approach the future? Dread, passivity, ambition, and creativity are ways. Dread is fear of the future and will likely lead to paralyzing inaction. Passivity means that one wants the future to be different but is not willing to do something in order to make it so. Ambition is the desire to force the world into producing a particular future, but the world will rarely comply without unforeseen consequences. Creativity means having goals but also possessing the openness to improvise when the world exerts its will upon you. Creativity is the constructive path. In it, there is the idea of creating yourself and creating things such as works of art. But creativity doesn't have the other forceful destructive aspects that "blind" ambition can acquire. The creative types, of course, are not beyond jealousy. Artists have a harder time fitting into the competitive world despite the fact that we have "Best of Show" awards. Many artists realize that art can't be competitive. Creativity means having a goal that one is aiming at and that may mean having to take a meandering path. The creative person does not mind wandering. He will find a way to get where he is going and will often stumble upon beauty along the way.

#20

To be prolific means to have low standards!

There is something about chasing inspiration and having the desire to capture the idea and then move on that is more powerful than crafting the project.

Prolific artists have a "catch and release" mentality—meaning they capture the idea and its essence, get it recorded, and release it so they can go on to the next fish. Their standards can't be too perfectionist and their work can't be too meticulous. If so, their work loses its spontaneity and ethereal nature. This quick capture approach does not mean that the work is not beautiful and profound. Some artists are not going to be able to invest their time into grooming the projects into the most mature work that might be possible. Music is actually an art form where the simple melody can be made more complex over time. Often artist's "Live Albums" are better than their studio albums because they have found more nuances in the melody over time. Even for prolific artists there will likely be a time when the ideas start to slow down, the projects start becoming more complicated, or the artist wants to explore a particular piece to its fullest possibilities. Some poems can be cleaned up years later and some artwork is not quite right. Each person has to work at their own pace and discover which pace works best for them. But you must capture the ideas when they arrive and then you can decide on how much investment you are willing to give each project.

#29

The significant people in your life are your muses.

There's a lot of thought about muses in this chapter. What is a muse? A muse is someone who inspires projects and someone who supports your endeavors when you are struggling. For the most part, they are real people but they can also be imaginary. They are people who you get ideas from. Sometimes they let you talk about your projects and don't interrupt. They might ask you particularly good questions that get you thinking about a potential next project. They can be a person who says, "I love your work, tell me what you were thinking when you came up with that?" They can be your one and only fan. A muse can be a person who believes in you and comes to your openings without being personally invited. A muse can be a dream character who you seek inspiration and affection from. A muse can be a person from your past who always said "deep stuff." A muse is someone who inspires you to work—not just inspires you, but inspires you to work.

#33

Remember that when you trip, you are usually in between steps.

When I was in high school I ran track for four years. I was pretty fast on the ground but I was better when half of me was on the ground and half was in the air so I became a hurdler. One race stands out in particular: I was winning a race in the 300 meter hurdles by a far stretch—which was unusual. As I cleared the second to last hurdle, I stumbled and got off balance. As I tried to clear the last hurdle, I tripped and fell down. I was so close to the finish line that I got up and dove for it at about the same time that the other runners were crossing. Officially, the announcer said that I had come in first place and the hometown crowd cheered for me because of the effort I exhibited in trying to complete the task. Later on, they changed the results so that I had placed second. No one groaned. No one seemed to even notice. It didn't really matter to them and it didn't matter to me. Success is a lot like this. I am reminded that you will fall on your face. I am reminded that you may stumble when you think you have it made. I am reminded that as an artist you are always between safety and danger. I hope that you will always get up and dive for the finish line. The next step is not out of your reach; it is just a little higher than your foot thought.

#37

In our culture when we feel inspiration we take Pepto-Bismol.

You'd probably be disappointed if you added up all the times you've heard or said, "That's a great idea, you should do something with it," and then saw how many times the project was actually pursued. Rarely is another person's acknowledgement of the worthwhile potential of an idea enough motivation to push us to begin that project. Instead, we tend to immediately squelch the possible project with a variety of excuses: "I'm too busy now;" "I'm sure someone has thought of that already;" "I don't have the know-how to pull it off." Creative work is often undermined and ignored from the very beginning. What is missed in all those excuses is that creative projects are *growth opportunities for one's imagination.* The more we honor those opportunities—the more likely they will present themselves to us. It's like learning a new word and then hearing people use it three times the very next day. If we worry too much about the outcome, we will never begin in the first place.

#45

We often think that passion is something you find or tap into rather than something you generate.

The desire to feel passionately about something is a deep drive in life. Like many elevated experiences, passion is also a difficult feeling to maintain. When there is an absence of passion in our lives, we often wonder how to find it. I imagine there are at least three approaches to the problem: passive seeking, actively-passive seeking, and active seeking. For the most part, passive seeking includes waiting for opportunities and hoping that the environment will provide sources of inspiration. This is probably the most frustrating since there is a sense of dependence on external events—although occasionally, passion *will* find you. The question is whether you will act upon it. Actively-passive seeking seems more eastern or Taoist in that one is constantly observing and searching but not necessarily forcing the issue. To search for passion is active because one is consciously seeking and attempting to absorb sources of passion without manipulating situations. Active seeking is more of a Western view. In it, one seeks, actively pursues, manipulates forces, uses grit, and makes ultimatums so as to push the forces that are present. Highs and many lows are likely to come from attempting to exert your will against things that are often out of your control. How, then, is passion generated? It comes by learning from yourself while working at your art. Each project that one works on can naturally spawn several others if we pay attention to the questions that our current project poses. The last project should reveal a weakness in technique, an issue with negative space, a symbol with a double meaning, a surface whose texture was not quite exhausted, and a new brush stroke. The front door is only the first door.

#49

Even artists must remember how to play.

The reason that children are good at playing is that they don't know the rules. Rules aren't real. They are made up. At best rules should be understood as guidelines; ideas you should follow, unless you have a reason to go against them. If you have a reason to ignore rules then do so, knowing that you are doing so. Play is freedom. Play is tasting-"Hmm, I don't like that one, let's try another. I don't like that ending. What else can we do?" Play means to bring the infinite to the actual. Play means to let intuition select the best fitting pattern out of the ones imagined and pick that as the intention. It means that ALL art is experimentation. If it works, your play was successful in most places. If it doesn't work, so what? You were experimenting; not everything is a masterpiece and not everything needs to be taken so seriously. Play is both a tempering of rules and a tempering of criticism. Play is letting go of expectations and taking a philosophy of: "Let's see what happens." It's not that the artist is not invested in the outcome; she wants the best possible turn out. The outcome is not a reflection of the artist's talents; rather, the artwork is its own being and the artist's ego is not at stake while playing.

#**52**

Never let the truth get in the way of your imagination. Truth is always a post-hoc evaluation.

The imagination is often over-burdened when we request Greatness, Truth, or Masterpieces. These are titles that are given by others and not by our selves. I shutter when I hear people say, "I want to write the next great novel." That's a lot of pressure to put on your imagination. The imagination is not a truth revealer as much as it is a truth bender. I have found myself recently repeating the comment: "I don't know if it is true, but it is interesting." The power of quality art and quality thinking has more to do with the sparks that the work produces in the viewers. Powerful work often wants to punch a hole in the truth or show that there might be something where others think there is nothing. It might be a hundred years before your art is true.

#54

I was only the key holder for a moment.

An artist is a un-locker. The artist has a key that allows you to have your perspective twisted. Each one of us needs some wrenching from time to time. A good artist gives us a quarter turn. A great artist shows us that he can give us several turns over time. What makes art so special is that it is not for mass consumption. A piece of art either speaks to you or it doesn't and when it speaks, you are captivated. Why is this beautiful to you or powerful or meaningful? Oftentimes, if you visit a gallery with a friend and you talk about a piece you can see why a piece of art is special to them. Keep that friend. Also, the art certainly will mean more to you than it did before. You will inherit some of the meaning of the piece from your viewer friend. An artist tries to hold the key to your heart and unlock it even for just a minute. That is the great service the artist provides.

All beauty fades quickly.

#57

Holding other people down is never a road to creative superiority, or superior creativity.

Art is like any other activity where success is rare and only a small percentage of people seem to rise to a level of recognition. It's hard to say what it is that allows a person to reach that success. I like to say that success and recognition are gained through hard work, unique content or perspective, and work that has different levels of intelligibility and wonderful basics like color or word choice. We do know sometimes worthy artists and musicians are not noticed, while other folks seem to mysteriously walk into the spotlight. Either way, we should be generous with our fellow artists and do what we can to keep them working on their projects. Everyone is out here trying to express himself or herself and yes, sometimes people walk into a fortunate situation without having any of the above ingredients. The true success of a person, I think, is really measured by how many artists you can pull up to another level with you. That is, how many other artists can you help with your time and insight. Can you lend an ear to a struggling artist, collaborate with someone who could ride on your coat tails, recognize the potential in some neophyte artist or in any way, help move forward someone who is stagnating. If success has not come your way, I suggest you try to help others in as genuine a way as possible and you might find that the success you seek may come to you through your progeny.

#64

Each day you should have at least one thought that is worth writing down.

If you could keep track of every thought you have in a day, certainly one of them would make you smile or think or laugh. Maybe one would be profound and another kind of strange. Isn't it amazing that many days pass and we go to bed without writing down a single idea, thought, or quip? This entire book is simply a collection of single thoughts that I have written down while working on my art projects or thinking about my art. I started writing them on scraps of paper; eventually, I started writing them down in journals. I often would write them on pieces of art that I had attributed to be trash. In my old house, I started writing them on the white walls of the coal seller. When we left that house, I took pictures of the walls because I had not transferred the statements into my journals. This is no special talent I have. I just realized at some point, "These are my thoughts and I like them. I'm going to capture them." The ones in this collection are about art. I have others about a host of different topics. Whenever I feel that I'm blocked or haven't made a piece of art in a while, I'll go back and read several pages of these thoughts. There are always ones that I find funny, profound, and others that are barely intelligible. In a few years from now, some of them likely will swap those characteristics. These are our daily 'transmissions' and we should honor their presence by writing them down.

#73

Creativity's death is boredom.

On any rainy day, if we are sequestered with a grade school child, we are inevitably going to hear the complaint, "I'mmmmm bored." This is largely a result of the fact that children for the first 15 or so years are largely constantly entertained and that entertainment comes from the outside; it is externalized amusement. Hopefully, we can teach our child the value of reading and maybe school can help the child learn to play with their imaginations during recess. But the fact is, the mind is the real playground. The adult learns that with a few simple questions a creative spark can start a whole forest fire of imaginings. In fact, anything that doesn't work well is an invention invitation. Any boring task begs the question, "How can I make a game out of any menial task?" In boredom, the person finds the self to be empty and looks to the familiar outside to provide the entertainment. Boredom is watching your self do nothing. Boredom is becoming aware of the lack of imagination in your life. Boredom is the revelation that you depend on other's imaginations for your own entertainment.

Creativity produces possibilities through inquiry. Every person is born creative. But we relinquish this often through school and through our TV culture, both of which constrict the development of our own imagination. Reinvigorating creativity is the task of adulthood. Finding a single project that is worth your time will usually produce a number of sacred side projects that will keep your artist's plate full. In most cases, the artist has to learn how to select the most worthy candidates and protect one's self from burn out because ideas are easy but the work is hard. An artist has to say no to some projects.

#83

Invite it! Welcome it! Enjoy it! Thank it! (*repeat*)!

This is a principle, not a formula, for receiving the artistic vision that you are seeking. It will probably work with a lot of other things in one's life. "Invite it!" means that you have to ask for what you want to come. You can't expect it to drop by without an invitation—that would be rude. By inviting what you want, you will be anticipating its arrival. "Welcome it!" means that when something arrives, make it known that you appreciate the fact that it has stopped by. Any guest or artistic insight that comes here is welcome—no judging, no closed doors. When a new thought comes to me, I write it down. I don't say, "That one is not worthy, or that one will make me look like a fool." I honor it by writing it down. "Enjoy it!" means that some transmission has come to you and your day is better because of it. You got a visit from an image, a lyric, a thought, or an insight. Any interactions of this kind are certainly better than loneliness. Thoughts are visitors. Enjoy their company for they will have to go soon. "Thank it!" means that when it leaves, make it known that the visit was valuable and that this company is welcomed back at any time. Thanking time is a good time to invite the guest back for another visit. This is how you get abundance. Cease this process if abundance becomes too much. But remember the process if you grow dry.

Author Biography

Dr. Richard Bargdill earned his PhD in clinical psychology from Duquesne University. Currently, Dr. Bargdill is an assistant professor of psychology at the Virginia Commonwealth University. He is editor and co-editor of two upcoming books: *Psychology and the Good Life: Selected Readings from the History of Psychology* and *Introduction to Humanistic Psychology: A Supplemental Text.* He is currently the Secretary and the Membership Chair for The Society for Humanistic Psychology (Division 32 of the American Psychological Association) and previously served as a board member. In 2014, he is invited go give the opening keynote address at the Third International Conference on Existential Psychology held in Guangzhou, China. In addition, Rich has won multiple awards for his poetry and visual artwork (but not his singing). His sculpture called "I'm a tree chopped down everyday" was recently awarded 1st place at the official Pennsylvania State Art show.

Other Books by University Professors Press

*The Polarized Mind: Why It's Killing Us and What
We Can Do About It*
by Kirk J. Schneider, PhD

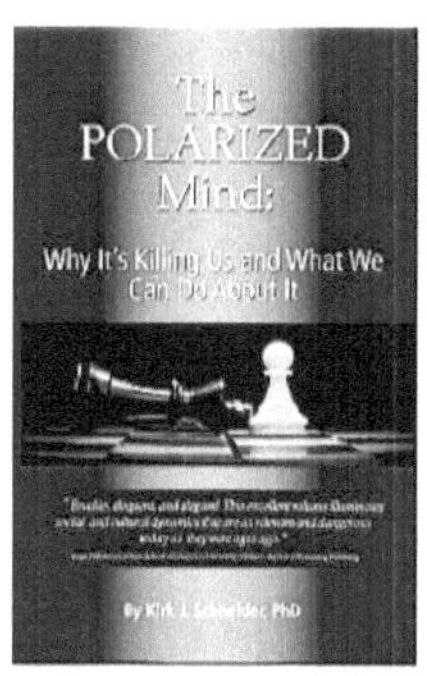

Bare: Psychotherapy Stripped
by Jacqueline Simon Gunn with Carlo DeCarlo

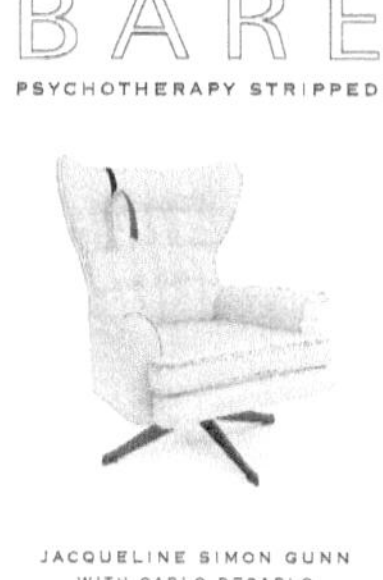

www.ingramcontent.com/pod-product-compliance
Lightning Source LLC
Chambersburg PA
CBHW031113250726
48655CB00004B/1697